DRESSED TO KILL
Sex Power and Clothes

DRESSED TO KILL

Sex Power & Clothes

COLIN McDOWELL

HUTCHINSON

London

For Dora and Jill Edmonds

© Colin McDowell 1992

The right of Colin McDowell to be identified as Author of this work has been asserted by Colin McDowell in accordance with the Copyright, Designs and Patents Act, 1988

This edition first published in 1992 by Hutchinson

Random Century Group Ltd
20 Vauxhall Bridge Road, London SW1V 2SA

Random Century Australia (Pty) Ltd
20 Alfred Street, Milsons Point, Sydney, NSW 2061, Australia

Random Century New Zealand Ltd
18 Poland Road, Glenfield, Auckland, New Zealand

Random Century South Africa (Pty) Ltd
PO Box 337, Bergvlei, 2012, South Africa

BRITISH LIBRARY CATALOGUING-IN-PUBLICATION DATA

McDowell, Colin
      Dressed to Kill: Sex Power and Clothes.
      1. Title
      391

ISBN 0-09-174464-4

Designed by Paul Bowden Design

Repro by Colorlito, Milan
Photoset in 10 pt Baskerville by 🔺 Tek Art Limited, Croydon, Surrey
Printed and bound in Great Britain by
Butler & Tanner Ltd, Frome and London

Contents

Acknowledgements

I have been helped by various people in the preparation of this book and have enjoyed many stimulating conversations with friends about the nature of fashion, the ramifications of power and the different forms of sexual attraction but, as always, there is some help that must be individually – and gratefully – acknowledged.

My greatest debt is to Timothy Cooke who not only typed the manuscript but also edited it as he went along. He was able to make many insightful comments that I was happy to include in the final version. I also owe a great debt to Rivers Scott and Brenda Polan for suggesting some important additions to the text. I am further indebted to Peter Farrer and Anne Brogden for their generosity with their time, scholarship and excellent library. Pat Murgatroyd did marvellous work finding apt and unusual quotations, for which I am grateful.

Special thanks must go to Elizabeth Wilson and Penelope Byrde, who read the manuscript and offered invaluable suggestions, many of which I was able to incorporate (although responsibility for the final version is entirely mine) and, finally, to my picture editor, Jenny de Gex, whose contribution was simply invaluable. The pictures are supplementary to the text and are not to be 'read' as illustrating points from it. Rather, they tell their own independent story.

Preface

Three episodes will explain why I have written this book. The first concerns the power that appearances have; the second shows how fashion has in recent years made itself easy to dismiss by disappearing into a cul-de-sac of fantasy, elevated self-regard and hype; and the third demonstrates the intellectual unease created in commentators by the paradox of the obvious importance of clothes and the trivial antics of the world in which they originate.

I am standing in New Bond Street, waiting to cross the road. I am aware of a couple hovering near an unattended parked car. He is tall and thin, with a weak, grey look to his face. His knees sag and his feet meet the ground at not quite the right angle. Were he older, he would shuffle. As it is, he does not look robust, even though he can only be in his late forties. She is small and stout, bespectacled and with the rosy pinkness that is romantically associated with country milk maids. She has no-nonsense calves and her feet are planted heavily, even wearily, on the ground. The couple would be unmenacing, even endearing and pathetic, were it not for the way they are dressed. For these people are traffic wardens, and their clothes counteract any sympathetic appearance they might have. When traffic-flow problems reached such proportions that wardens were required, the uniform chosen for them in Britain was black and yellow. These, as every schoolboy knows, are nature's colours of aggression. Wasps and tigers – things that sting and bite – are coloured thus in order to warn and to inspire fear. The wardens' yellow and black striped hats signalled that their intended role was not to help the motorist, but to harry and punish. Even the police – themselves seen as either helpers or harriers, according to one's age, colour and creed – are not dressed in such a crudely aggressive way. No wonder, with such an uncompromising and obvious colour scheme, that motorists soon learned to loathe and fear the traffic warden. What would have been the reaction if, instead of black and yellow, traffic wardens had been dressed entirely in yellow? The menace would at once have been dispelled, and traffic wardens would have become not merely friendly, but even slightly ludicrous, clown-like figures. They would be obeyed by nobody. Simplistic as the black and yellow message might be, it is effective; an example of twentieth-century power dressing that works.

I am sitting among a tense and expectant audience in the courtyard of the *Académie des Beaux Arts* in Paris. We are waiting and watching. We are waiting for the house of Chanel to show its collection of ideas as to how women should dress in the coming spring and summer. We are waiting because it is almost traditional that the audience of international press, buyers, manufacturers and suppliers must be humbled a little by having it brought home to them that the Maestro is a superior being, not to be harassed by a vulgar crowd; a being who will commence his show when *he* feels he should. We are waiting in the unlikely expectation that here at Chanel a fashion bombshell will be dropped which, like Dior's New Look in 1947, will make all other fashion irrelevant. Fashion is eternally hopeful.

We are watching, because that is how fashion folk are impelled to spend much of their time. Because their world is amorphous and transitory, they are riven with insecurities. Is one 'in' or 'out' is a question that is asked almost daily. One of the best ways of judging – especially for journalists – is to notice one's placing at fashion shows. I am well back, along with many other British journalists. Far in front of us, the icily polite Chanel PRs have placed editors in chief, publishers and owners of magazines, along with their girl- and boy-friends, in the belief that they will influence the coverage their magazines will give to the show. The journalists here to report on the clothes can see nothing of the models below waist level, whilst their bosses, here for social show and enjoyment alone, can see everything.

The show begins. The grey melancholy of autumnal Paris is banished as the courtyard explodes with colour, light and music.

Chanel clothes are designed by the German Karl Lagerfeld, a man of protean talents who holds a dominant position in international fashion. As the models skip down the runway in revealing chiffon skirts, little-girl straw hats and a plethora of extraneous jewellery and accessories, I think of how Coco Chanel would have despised this tasteless display. It is ironic that, forced to flee into exile after the Second World War because she had openly been the mistress of a high-ranking German officer, Chanel should now have her memory torn apart by another German who, like a modern stormtrooper, has jack-booted his way through her philosophy of how women should appear in the twentieth century. As the show piles excess on excess, it is hard to recall that this is the house founded on a belief that clothes should never degenerate into fancy dress.

'Clothes must be logical,' the ghost of Coco Chanel moans in despair above the raucous music and loud cheers from an audience which is looking for bread and circuses, not fashion.

I am reading through the critical comment on a television programme I made in 1991 on the *couturier* Christian Dior. It was part of a series reassessing the reputations of writers such as Virginia Woolf, composers such as Benjamin Britten, and painters such as Van Gogh, and was the first arts programme to look seriously at a fashion figure. For that reason, it made commentators nervous and disorientated. The arts are, in common wisdom, serious; fashion is frivolous. People are embarrassed and rather afraid to take seriously anything to do with dress and appearance. This fear shows in the reviews of the programme. They reveal a jokey dismissal of the preposterous idea that anyone should actually be asked to view fashion in terms of sociological effect or artistic power. 'A storm in an elegant tea cup,' opines the *Daily Mail*; 'Like hitting a meringue with a crowbar,' reacts the *Observer*. Such patronising and dismissive comments on the subject rather than the approach are the normal reaction when fashion attempts to come out of the salon and asks to be thought about by intelligent people. All but the most enlightened consider such a move pretentious and even arrogant – a frock is a frock is a frock . . . until, sanctified by the years, it becomes costume, and finally worthy of intellectual appraisal.

Fear of society, fear of oneself, fear of the power of clothing; fear is the reason fashion is so often dismissed as flippant and foolish. Such a dismissal is made all the easier by the behaviour of those for whom fashion is important. They frequently *are* foolish and flippant. It is easy to discount them and, by doing so, to relegate fashion to a ghetto without values, impervious to critical assessment, where pretty frocks are 'to die for' and extravagance (of thought, gesture and creativity) becomes an end in itself. Such a dismissal occurs every day in the lives of thinking people afraid to address the question of dress in all its ramifications. Intelligent interest in clothing has been pushed aside by the majority of society, and *Dressed to Kill* aims to discover why.

In researching this book I have leaned heavily on the published work of Aileen Ribeiro and her scholarly band of graduates from the Courtauld Institute. In the last few years their discoveries have been given radical interpretations by sociology lecturers in colleges and polytechnics – known collectively and not unkindly as the North London Sisterhood. Elizabeth Wilson is a seminal figure here. The rigour of these two quite separate scholarly approaches has done much to rid fashion history and comment of the influence of Laverism, which so often seemed to eschew facts in favour of the broadly sweeping generalisation producing nicely buttoned-up theories. Although frequently factually correct in broad terms, such an approach destroys itself by squeezing everything into the corset of a well-turned aphorism or a preconceived notion.

Dressed to Kill is deliberately discursive. It crosses the divides of past and present, male and female, youth and age many times in each chapter. My intention has been to break down barriers, highlight correspondences and follow a flow of thought. To the rigidly minded who might find it 'all over the place', I send my condolences but not my apologies. To those who feel it is neither a fashion nor a sociological book, I can only concur. That was the intention. There are enough of both already. To the lover of fair play who accuses me of being partisan, I can merely say that I absolutely agree. I hope that this book might provide a little irritation, some discussion and perhaps a move away from the knee-jerk attitudes assumed by intelligent people when fashion is mentioned.

ONE

Male and Female Architecture

Sex is a twentieth-century invention. Love and lust are as old as mankind itself, but the exploitation of them for commercial gain – apart from prostitution – is comparatively new, and it was that exploitation that gave rise to the concept of sex. Whereas love and lust can be quite separate from dress – although they rarely are – sex and clothing are inextricably linked. Clothes are not just the armour of the class war; they are the uniform for the battle of the sexes. Bared female shoulders lead the eye to the twin peaks of passion which are exciting because, in contrast, they are not exposed. Clothed male legs act as twin conduits to the source of desire. A woman naked from the waist up and a man nude from the waist down might well excite some interest, but it is more likely to be social than sexual. The onlooker will be less intrigued by the what of the exposure than the why.

Social discomfort through sexual mistakes hits us all. Puritanical attitudes are so engrained that we are embarrassed if the body or even its intimate clothing is exposed in a way not sanctified by our culture. In *The Psychology of Clothes* J.C. Flügel went further and referred to all clothes as 'a perpetual blush upon the surface of humanity'. They have a great potential for creating social unease, which is why we consider certain items of dress acceptable only in specific places or times. Women who sunbathe topless at the beach are ashamed if their slip shows in the city; men who wear cut-away vests exposing their torsos are horrified if they forget to fasten their flies. Erogenous zones are as precise as they are illogical. They are of two kinds: the permanent, specifically reproductive, and the shifting, whereby changing parts of the body become fashionable at different times as sexual stimulants.

Our dress must always speak in a standard tongue, respecting that which is allowed to be shown and that which must be hidden. To dress otherwise is the equivalent of swearing. Even the dress of the young – the slang of fashion – bows to the taboos even as it appears to outrage them. Young men and women wearing jeans slit across the thighs and buttocks to reveal another layer beneath know full well the 'you think you see it, but you don't' game they are playing. By splitting their jeans across areas that society demands must be covered, they appear to be defying the rules but, by wearing a second layer, they show that they are as hidebound by convention as the rest of us. After the first frisson of shock (or even anticipation) such craven conformity makes the initial boldness seem pathetically lacking in courage as a gesture against society. Those who find bared buttocks an excitement have merely to go for gratification to the beach, where minute bikinis and posing slips – revealing that which exposing away from the beach would result in arrest – show the illogicality of our prudery.

As costume historian C. Willett Cunnington pointed out, we are reluctant to abandon prudery because it provides 'endless aphrodisiacs'. But that is only part of the question.

Prudery is a form of censorship and control. Its purpose is to subject the individual to the rule of society. It is illogical, like the old sumptuary laws conceived by kings to control the aspirations of commoners by debarring them from wearing certain colours and materials. That a woman's breasts can be seen on the beach but not on the bus shows how strange and unpredictable prudery is. The child of prudery is modesty – a state as difficult to justify as it is to quantify. It is found neither in the animal kingdom, nor among primitive peoples, but it has been part of Western society ever since that society was first formalised.

Social intercourse is based on self-projection. We reach out with our personalities through speech and action and we dress in order to express those personalities too. But even those whose personalities, speech and actions are most immodest conform to the rules of prudery when it comes to modesty of dress. We wish to display our bodies but are prepared to do so only within tightly prescribed limits. Society is so afraid of the power of the body that it protects us by law from those who wish to flaunt areas of flesh considered too dangerous to be seen by anyone not on the most intimate of terms with them. In mid-Victorian times, men bathed nude as a matter of course but later periods have been more prudish – until the advent of nude beaches in the seventies – and any area of the body primarily considered specific to sexuality had to be covered in public. The nude craze that flowered after the first few brave souls bared all showed just how constraining society's rules had been and how out of touch with many people's real needs they had become. All rules lag behind the reality of the moment, but our sexual rules are especially slow to change. The law continued to consider nudity a crime long after topless bathing had become so commonplace that it hardly raised an eyebrow on most Continental beaches.

Even male nudity has gained ground, although less so in Britain than elsewhere, and universally less widely than female nudity. The unroused male penis, pink and pathetic, is as unlikely to raise any emotion (apart from mirth) as the male bottom is to excite uncontrollable desire in the female onlooker. Viewed dispassionately, it is hard to imagine why society has, for so long, been determined to keep genitalia covered except in the bedroom and the sexually segregated bath house. Sir Richard Burton claimed, in *The Anatomy of Melancholy*, that 'the greatest provocation of lust comes from apparel.' If he is correct, why does nudity create such alarm among those who consider it their duty and their right to protect us from ourselves and indoctrinate us with feelings of revulsion at our lust for certain parts of the bodies of strangers? If he is correct, why are the breasts of Page Three girls exposed, and not enclosed in erotically suggestive clothing? If he is correct, why are men so reluctant to pose naked for women's magazine?

Whereas the female body can be exposed totally naked in magazines and films, the male nude is normally presented in clothes that hide the genitals and are, in themselves, a shorthand for sexuality: brief underpants, frayed jeans, leather pants, rubber wet suits or Lycra cycling shorts. Such pictures acknowledge that, in the case of the male anatomy, anticipation is more exciting than actuality. In most cases, as the editors of gay porno magazines are aware, the male penis is only of interest when aroused. Although society feels that, within strict limits of sales availability, male homosexuals can be exposed to the sight in magazines, women cannot – any magazine publisher who put on general release pictures of the aroused male would immediately be arrested. The charge would be that, by doing so, he had, in some mysterious way, threatened public order.

The traditional justification for controlling all male nudity and banning aroused male nudity was that women found it distasteful. Men have long harboured the convenient illusion that dirty thoughts are exclusively a male privilege, and that the sight of male flesh would bring a well brought up woman to her bed with the vapours. Whereas an uprightly, downrightly, forthrightly decent man might enjoy the sight of female flesh belonging to strangers, decent women, it was felt, not only did not but actually could not do so with the male body. Female sexuality, received wisdom runs, is different: covert, not overt, as male sexuality is; emotional, not sensual. It was untrue even in Victorian times, when men bathing nude in public usually gathered a crowd of female admirers who enjoyed the sight even as they pretended to avert their gaze. The lie has persisted so long that even some women still believe it. But it remains a lie, as anyone who has listened to women talking or watched and listened to them at male fashion shows or, even more revealingly, a male strip show, can testify. Female speculation in offices as to the size of the Lycra-clad courier's member; screams of 'Get 'em off' as the stripper stands in his bejewelled briefs: these are not the signs of women attempting to ape the strident sexuality of their male 'betters'. They are the sounds of a sex that has finally come back into its own, after centuries of male subjugation, as being as sensual as its counterpart – indeed, perhaps even more so.

Female modesty was invented and imposed by men to protect their own dignity – and male dignity is firmly rooted in the penis. The message was simple: don't call us, we'll call you. Women could not instigate sex. They had no right to want the penis; they were there merely to receive it when it wanted them. It was the man who decided when the time for sex had come, and it was his roused penis that showed it. It was a treat, reserved as a reward, but also a threat, kept as a punishment. It was the most important thing in male-female relationships, and women were not allowed to forget that or their lack of control over its use. Crudely exposed in the fourteenth century; ludicrously exaggerated in the fifteenth; beguilingly hidden in the sixteenth; sexily hinted at in the seventeenth; wantonly outlined in the eighteenth; and cunningly suggested in the nineteenth, the penis has always been central to male fashion. Women were kept constantly aware that between a man's legs hangs his weapon, as he revealingly christens it, to chastise and hurt them when he wishes. It is also his tool – a mechanical device to unlock, ease and work the female sexual mechanism at his will.

Of course, the power of the penis is yet another male myth which man acknowledged long ago by creating another. The guilty weight of sexuality was too much for him to bear. He had to transfer it and so he created the image of the woman as wanton, the Jezebel who lured him into sin. As early as AD 347, Saint John Chrysostom was berating her as 'a necessary evil, a natural temptation, a desirable calamity, a deadly fascination and a painted ill'. Swinburne in 1866 wrote of the sinister temptress with her

Cold eyelids that hide like a jewel,
Hard eyes that grow soft for an hour,
The heavy white limbs, and the cruel
Red mouth like a venomous flower

The Jezebel has long been a star player in the charade of the sexes. In one of history's breathtakingly slick-wristed sleights of hand, man paraded himself as the potential victim, desperately holding closed the floodgate of female sexuality that, without his constraints, would burst open and swamp civilisation. The moral outrage went on for centuries. John Knox in *The First Blast of the Trumpet Against the Monstrous Regiment of Women* in 1558 hit out at abominable and odious gorgeous female apparel. The hysterical puritan Philip Stubbes became almost crazy with anger at gorgeousness of dress in his *The Anatomie of Abuses* in 1585, where he castigated all extravagant clothing but, predictably, reserved his true invective for women who, fashionably dressed, were 'but artificiall women, not women of flesh and bloude, but rather puppits or mawmets . . . '

Pride, the deadly sin, became perceived as a female failing, despite the extravagance of male dress in the sixteenth and seventeenth centuries. In *Dr Faustus*, it boasted that it could 'creep into every corner of a wench'. Thomas Reeve in *God's Plea for Nineveh* (1657) was appalled at the extravagance and artifice of women, exclaiming 'Oh, these birds of Paradise are bought at a dear rate! . . . The wife oftentimes doth wear more gold upon her back than the husband hath in his purse . . . and this is the she-pride.' He continues, 'And doth not the he-pride equal it? Yes, the man is now become as feminine as the woman.'

The wickedness of male peacockery has always been laid at woman's door. This is a guilt even greater than her sin of sexual enticement. By her ostentatious appearance she encourages man to be as vain and extravagant as she is. It is no slip of the pen when Stubbes calls 'Apparrell and Pride . . . the mother and daughter of mischief', rather than the father and son. Society is constructed by males for males. If women, by their vainglorious dress, lay sexual traps for men, it follows that gorgeously attired men are even more dangerous. That is why effeminate men have always been ridiculed by their own sex. To accept that they are attractive would be to run the risk of seeming *homosexually* attracted to them. Appalled at the idea that men could be naturally effeminate, society looked for a scapegoat for behaviour dubbed deviant and found it in women, the age-old sexual seducers. It was their blatantly sexual dress that encouraged men to be equally shameless, ran the theory. It was yet another example of sin-shifting.

The fundamental fashion split that showed man's fear of female sexuality had taken place even before Stubbes and the puritanical paranoids. Primitive societies had early realised the superior sexual importance of the female. It was only as civilisation advanced that acknowledging it – and its corollary, the insignificance of the male whose role in the furtherance of the species is so fleeting – became a sexual problem. The male did not want his woman to be shared promiscuously in case, by such experience, she learnt of his inadequacy. He acknowledged her inferior sex and superior sexuality by wishing to preserve and protect her from other men. The concept of exclusivity was born, and its camouflage was modesty. The ideal cloak for such modesty was the skirt. Long and all-enveloping, it was the antithesis of dress as sexual stimulant.

Tailoring requires skills that draping does not, and it is tempting to assume that those societies where men continued to wear what to modern eyes appear as skirts – Mayan Indians, Greeks, Hungarian peasants, even Highlanders – did so because they lacked those skills. Even more tempting would be the hope that they had avoided the sexual stereotypes that engulfed the rest of us. In reality, however, they were merely acknowledging the practical superiority of the wrap-around garment over a bifurcated covering such as trousers. There is nothing essentially sexual in the consideration. As Eric Gill, the twentieth century's apologist for the skirt for men, has said, 'the skirt is not especially a female architecture nor the trouser a male.' He could have added that, if anything skirts are more accommodating to the male physique than trousers. As he points out, 'men are neither more nor less in need of modesty than women . . . women are neither more nor less legged than men . . . if skirts are suitable for women, they are also suitable for men.'

Skirts became taboo for men once they were established as primarily female dress. So great was the fear of the feminine taint that they rapidly became *exclusively* female dress.

As a corollary, it was taboo for Western women, with the exception of the lowest level of worker, to imitate men by wearing male garb. The Old Testament codifies the law: 'A woman shall not wear that which pertaineth unto a man, neither shall a man put on a woman's garment; for whosoever doeth these things is an abomination unto Jehovah thy God.' Stubbes, predictably, holds a strong view. 'Our apparrell', he writes in *The Anatomie of Abuses*, 'was given as a signe distinctive to discerne betwixt sexe and sexe; and, therefore, one to weare the apparrell of another sexe is to participate with the same, and to adulterate the verity of his own kinde.' As late as Victorian times, the moral taboo remained. A letter signed by 'An Admirer of "Women"' was published in a popular woman's magazine in 1889 protesting that 'The masculine shirt, tie, links, studs and collar, and a jacket or blazer may be all very well on the manly form but, I ask you, are they suitable for girls? . . . Mannish girls may attract a good deal of attention but they are not the sort of persons men select when choosing a partner for life . . . the fair charmers can "dress themselves to kill" without trespassing on the fashions of us masculines.'

That dress is burdened with so many moral provisos is a proof of its power and significance within society. In clear contradiction of the fact, many writers have persisted in denigrating an interest in fashion as proof of vanity, vacuity, or worse, and are critical of those who take more than a fleeting interest in appearance. It takes a radical reformer to buck the trend. G.B. Shaw's conversation with Lawrence Langner, author of *The Importance of Wearing Clothes*, in which he roundly condemned those who take up moral attitudes is as refreshing as it is perceptive: 'The trouble with these men who try to adjudicate upon what is moral or immoral in dress is that they really know nothing about the subject. Any man who attempts to decide that one style of clothing is seductive while another style of clothing is not, must know something about the art of being seductive, and priests who rail about women's costumes are obviously the very last persons to be in a position to express an opinion on the subject.' He ends with a typically Shavian flourish: 'There are really only two competent judges of what is seductive in women's clothing, and they are the women who make it their business to be seductive . . . and playwrights like myself, because it is our business to *know* what women must wear in order to be seductive.'

But moralists remain and the question that most exercises both them and costume commentators is the age-old one of whether the body is more seductive clothed or unclothed. If the latter, what purpose is there in fashion? We might as well all wear exactly the same style. If the former, what elements of clothing are most seductive? Fashion dresses the uncertainties and insecurities of the age, whilst highlighting its desires and aspirations. The longed-for state in a normal rather than a fetishistic congress, homo- or heterosexual, is surely nudity. However, nudity viewed outside passion is normally only attractive if the body conforms to the current ideal of physical beauty and sex appeal. In this century there has been a radical reappraisal of what constitutes sexual attraction.

As recently as Edwardian times, the attractive woman was the voluptuous woman. She was well-padded and she was not young. Some of the most successful *grandes horizontales* were well into middle age when they reached the peak of their careers. Such women were never tanned and prided themselves on the creaminess of their skin. The archetypal Edwardian man was burly, usually bearded and, again, of a certain age. Younger versions, the Mashers, were slimmer and normally wore only moustaches. In both sexes, the ideal of sexual perfection striven for was an upper middle-class one. Nobody wished to look like a member of the working classes.

Since the so-called Youth Quake in the sixties, middle-aged women have been thrown into sexual limbo, creamy female skin betokens the poverty that precludes foreign travel and the admired figure closely resembles that of a male adolescent in that, although it must be curvy and possess prominent breasts, it must carry no extraneous flesh. The male ideal is youthful, slim but muscular, the body of the man who works physically hard (or works out): direct, tough and unstoppable.

The age of sexual attractiveness has dropped dramatically. Fashion designers, photographers and the art editors of fashion magazines are in love with youth, even pre-pubescence. The search for the flawless virgin culminated in the late eighties. I recall being in a fashion photographer's studio watching him choose models from their photographic cards. He passed by a particularly beautiful face. When I asked why, he replied 'She's twenty-two, far too old. She would be working with a sixteen-year-old girl and it would be too cruel. Her age would show.' That particular slump into fashion paedophilia was short-lived, but its underlying conviction that mature beauty is flawed beauty persists.

We are all so deeply ashamed of vanity and so obsessed with our fear of ageing that we hide both under a carapace of care for society. We diet, jog and exercise because, we pretend, we wish to remain fit and efficient, able to pull our weight (preferably reduced) in our community and not become a drag on our fellows or a burden on the medical and welfare services. It is a lie. We do so because years of indoctrination have convinced us that the attractive body is the youthful one, lithe and healthy and, above all, slim. The cynical comment by the Duchess of Windsor that 'you can never be too rich or too thin' was the banner bright behind which lined up heterosexuals and homosexuals alike during the fashion-conscious eighties. The austere nineties might well demand circumspection as far as riches are concerned, but the slim figure remains the only figure for fashion. That is why, as Quentin Bell pointed out, billions of dollars which 'might be spent on making the thin fatter are devoted to making the fat thinner'. Modern criteria of beauty and sexual attractiveness are unbending: to be overweight is unattractive, and to be fat is repulsive. Those who wish to be taken seriously by fashion must contrive as best they can to look like twenty-year-olds.

The sweet dream of youth has been with us since the sixties, but it was in the early eighties that the age of fashion perfection dipped so alarmingly. Fashion is to do with the mood of the moment, and it is unwise to attempt to pinpoint its facets too precisely. Nevertheless, the first manifestation of pre-pubescence was provided by John Galliano, the London designer, in 1983, when the highpoint of his show was a group of extremely young girls wearing dampened white muslin and with ivy in their hair. Mad and from the world of faerie, like latter-day Ophelias or Titanias, they drifted ethereally down the catwalk, their breasts like tiny rosebuds. The woman had gone; the moment of the girl had arrived. Model competitions were won by fourteen-year-olds; fashion editors dressed twelve-year-olds in couture outfits, and the editor of British *Elle* felt it necessary to embargo the use of any model under sixteen. The shapeless, sexless figure of the unformed child fitted with the current mood for androgyny that had designers showing men in skirts and young men wearing make-up. The Milanese designer Romeo Gigli commercialised the mood and created child-women with virginally downcast eyes, narrow sloping shoulders and breasts bound flat, who tiptoed fearfully down his catwalk, unsmiling, like modern Infantas, simultaneously aware of their sexuality and alarmed by its vulnerability.

As the decade progressed, a similar slide in age occurred with men. The sexy body – and men's bodies were increasingly paraded in advertisements and actuality as sex objects – became the young body. Muscular but boyish, whippet-thin but tough, the male icon was allowed none of the heaviness of the mature man. That they were not yet men was acknowledged in their titles: Toy Boy and Rent Boy passed into the language and, indeed, into society. The first were wanted as sexual playthings for women, the second for men. Successful women in their middle years were happy to be seen on the arms of boys barely out of their teens, the equivalent of the businessman and his sexy young girlfriend, a couple who had been around for a long time, although she was now known as a Bimbo. Rent Boys sold their bodies in the secret world of every major city's homosexual underbelly. Here, youth was even more at a premium. A report in the *Guardian* in April 1990 pointed out the brief working life of male prostitutes. Like female fashion models, their careers usually ended before they were twenty-five. The report confirmed that the younger the boy, the higher his earnings from prostitution – as much as £500 per night for twelve-year-olds.

The whole feel of the movement towards youth and, increasingly, towards the male as sex object came together in the advertisements for Levi 501 jeans. They captured the sexual power of the pretty young man – still half boy – whilst allowing the shadow of his vulnerability in a corrupt and adult world. Of more interest was their sinister use of the young female. Suddenly we were back to Victorian standards – very much as we were with the Rent Boy boom. Woman was expected to be an adoring handmaiden to the young man, watching from the sidelines, impressed and excited by his cool cheek and sexual cockiness, waiting to be called forward when he was ready to share his triumphant self-confidence with her. The Levi 501 advertisements drove home the point that although women in what Simon Faulks called the 'Up Yours' Thatcher years might wear flame-coloured dresses, drive GTis and drink champagne together in wine bars, the world – and especially the sexual world – was still a male-dominated one.

It showed itself to be so, in a different form, with homosexuals. The eighties saw the virtual demise of the mincing pansy. The limp-wristed falsetto 'screaming queen', who had been such a comfort to heterosexual men because so different from normal manhood as to present no threat or suggest anything in common with a 'real' man, slowly disappeared. Homosexuals no longer answered to women's names or referred to each other as 'she'. They swung to the other extreme, dressing tough in jeans, leather jackets and tartan shirts, cropping their hair and wearing 'macho' Mexican moustaches. Rather than welcome the move, the 'straight' man felt frightened by the new, overtly masculine homosexual. He felt insecure in his own sexuality because the safe barrier of effeminacy – quite uncrossable for normally sexed men – had been torn down. Semiotic signals no longer meant anything. Anybody could be mistaken for a poofter now that sartorial pointers had gone. The dress of the majority of young homosexuals was almost indistinguishable from that of the majority of young men, as was their behaviour, outside the bedroom. Straight men actually began to copy homosexual styles and leather became commonplace.

With the increased youthful intolerance of sexual hypocrisy, kinkiness came out of the closet and bondage dressing was not only worn in public but featured by top fashion magazines such as *Vogue* and *Elle* as high-style clothing. Tight-lacing and corsetry have always been central to bondage games. Even the Victorians openly accepted their erotic quality. A letter in *Modern Society* for 7 October 1893, asked, 'What woman of taste, indeed, does not delight in the delicious creak of a satin stay?' Women were assumed to enjoy an erotic 'charge' from the discomfort and even the pain of tight corsetry. Men, it was also assumed, obtained their frisson of sexual excitement from knowing that pain was being inflicted, and the more sadistic enjoyed the thought that the corsets removed at night were frequently stained with blood. The garment as punishment was not new,

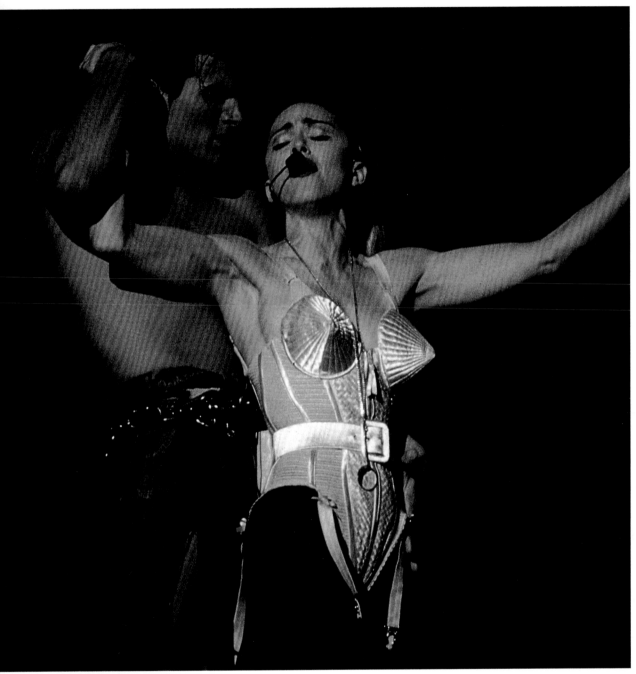

THRUSTING OUT

Did Jean Paul Gaultier have a nanny who undressed in front of him when he was very young? How else can his prurient obsession with corsetry be explained? It may well be the designer's dream to see young men walk the streets in padded codpieces but the important question is why is his vision not shared by most men? Does Gaultier see a link between today and the skintight fashions of young men in the fifteenth century – or does he work on nothing deeper than the truism that to shock brings notoriety, which soon converts to fame and – as every designer knows – that brings wealth. If so, he is perfectly in tune with Madonna who briefly used his underwear fashion to further her career by shocking middle class sensibilities. Although Gaultier's cone breasts were arresting they were not what gave the singer her look of raunchy sexuality. That came from the corset seaming that emphasised her crotch and made it fashion's erogenous zone of the early nineties.

BREAKING THE MOULD

Pam Hogg, a London designer who takes a radical view of sex, deplores stereotypes and believes that good taste is dead. Wearing cycling shorts and leggings, her models are 'Voguing' – that is, striking exaggerated fashion poses of the kind seen in glamorous fashion magazines in the fifties, and normally associated with women. 'Voguing' reveals the limitation of male sexual movements. As a 'come-on' men are forced to use female body language because their own culture provides none.

SEXUAL STANCES

Allure is about movement, gesture and stance. It has little to do with outright sex. Almost entirely a manifestation of thirties' film culture, allure did not reflect a sexual mood of the time: it tried to create one. Dietrich's seductive pose would be impossible for a modern woman – as would her dress, all airy illusion and pubic fluffiness. Monroe's appearance was a fantasy that lives on today only as an icon for transvestites who are attracted to figure-hugging gowns with lots of glitter. In fact, the fifties' originals were remarkably decorous, with skilfully placed embroidery and strategic jewelled clasps to ensure that they passed the censor's sharp eyes. Despite their seductive satins and tightly outlined figures, modern stars like Kim Basinger project an image that suggests that far, from attracting sex, they have already had it and have not been so terribly thrilled by the experience.

PACKAGED FOR PLAY

Hugh Heffner's Bunny Girls popped out from the pages of 'Playboy'. They were to be looked at, not touched, but the men who read the magazine and visited the club did not want to touch: they needed the fantasy of sex rather than the messy reality. The Playboy movement was anti-female in its cold distancing of women, as if they were objects – an idea made reality in the misogynist sculptures of Allen Jones. The Chippendales are the Bunny Girls' male equivalent in every sense except that the audience at a Chippendales show is usually laughing at itself as well as the performers.

HOME ON THE RAUNCH

Female raunchiness was the 'great' new discovery of fashion designers and photographers in the late eighties. They created a new stereotype for women in the hope that they would share mens' excitement at the crudely sexist exploitation of the female body.

of course. Stays have always been cruel, and yet women, through vanity or fear of appearing unfashionable – and therefore unattractive – have always worn them. Much apparent criticism of their cruelty was in fact written to titillate, as a letter in *The Queen* of 5 July 1852, makes clear: 'How one longs', it reads, 'to cut (once and forever) those hateful cords and let the pretty birds loose.'

What was different in the heated climate of Victorian middle-class life was the use of corsets for children of both sexes, as a punishment and a training. There were children's corsets for night as for day and, from Victorian popular magazines which dwelt lovingly on the necessity of chastisement for the young, it is apparent that corsets were frequently used as a form of child sexual abuse. The correspondence pages of these magazines verge on the pornographic, as punishments involving the use of corsets are described. They were, with their feminine connotations, considered especially apt for little boys. So rampant was masculinity in the spirit of the age that to turn a boy into a girl was the final, perfect degradation in order to tame his wildness. Girls who needed chastisement were, significantly, humiliated by being dressed as babies.

In *Men in Petticoats*, his fascinating selection of letters from Victorian newspapers, Peter Farrer has collected some of the more arcane examples of the Victorian misuse of dress as punishment. Whether or not all of the letters are genuine is arguable, but the need for them is clear from the great popularity of 'problem' correspondence of this kind. Stories of boy-maids were common, but the most revealing are those purporting to be first-hand accounts such as 'A Male Wasp-Waist', who wrote in *The Family Doctor* of 1886, 'Nothing is more pleasant or comfortable than a tight pair of good satin corsets. I love them and love to spend an hour in lacing and unlacing mine.' Another, signing himself 'Martyr', confesses that being brought up 'by an aunt who had a strong prejudice against boys', he was 'every morning and evening tightly laced into dainty satin corsets', to his evident satisfaction.

That men found corsets irresistibly exciting is apparent but so did many women who submitted to tight-lacing because they were convinced that it made them more alluring. The slightest exercise, when they were laced up, caused their breathing to become tremulous, and set their lace, bows and ribbons fluttering seductively. This is, perhaps, why Victorian women loved so much fussiness floating around their persons. As 'Mousie', writing in *Modern Society* in 1894, said, 'A girl without frills or flamees would be like a flower without foliage.' Another writer in the same publication pointed out that, 'the frou-frou of a skirt is, for a woman, music to her soul.'

To modern eyes, the fashion drawings and costumes from the period reveal only the monumentality of the shape of Victorian female dress, and not its sexual charge. Fashion writers and correspondents of the time repeatedly drew attention to the erotic sound of Victorian dress, something which does not exist in modern fashion, and of the power of which we are unaware. Victorian women did not put on their clothes and forget them. They chose their fabrics with care and orchestrated them – especially in undergarments – to give 'the expensive rustle of silk underskirts'. 'There is a fascination about really good satin . . . really fine, stiff satin makes a nice noise when you breathe,' a 'Female Flirt' wrote in *Modern Society* in 1893, 'An Empire bodice with great big sleeves will make a lovely lot of most fascinating noise, when you breathe or sigh; there is always something very catchy about a girl's breathing: the soft lift and fall of lace has always been confusing *and* alluring to a fellow, but we now have combined with this, a vague creasing sound, as if very crisp rose leaves were being crinkled.' Another writer in the same publication confessed 'to a decided weakness for fine feathers and fine birds, and in my secret soul delight in the soft rustle of silken skirts', a delight shared by men, who had in their own dress permanently thrown out the rustle of soft materials that they had enjoyed in the eighteenth century.

This was the true language of clothes and, to a certain extent, of sex too. But beneath the gracious choreography of the fashions, the tyranny of the corset was always present. Modern feminists see it as a garment of shame, shackling women for the pleasure of man, but it is apparent that much of the time it was a shared pleasure. Even today the corset has an ambivalent status. When Vivienne Westwood, Jean-Paul Gaultier and Madonna use corsets on top of clothes, is it to show that modern woman is in charge of her own sexuality and able to make her own decisions over constraints, discomfort, pain and fashion, or is it taking a fetish object out of the world of secret sex in order to tell us that the secret is not so terrifying after all and can now be openly enjoyed as a mild fetish object?

Fetishism is largely a masculine interest with little appeal for women – except as a way of exciting their men. That it is the only form of modern dress where sound is an important part of the sensation links it with Victorian dress. For the fetishist, excitement is not only to be found in the shininess of black latex or the way it clings. It is the 'swishing, rustling, slicking' noise that the clothes make which turns the fetishist on – what has been described as 'mackintosh music'. Maurice North, in *The Outer Fringe of Sex*, quotes a fetishist as saying 'the best material of all is plain cotton mackintosh, with all the rubber inside, it's so suggestive, and at the same time so sensual against one's own body. And the noise it makes is more subtle – the smell too.'

Rubber and leather are the fetishist's world, but they are augmented by satin, silk and fur, high-heeled shoes, fishnet stockings, capes, masks and hoods. According to North, by dressing from head to toe in rubber and wearing a mask, rubber fetishists are attempting to turn themselves into a penis and fulfil Freud's conclusion that fetishism is 'an abnormality, a sexual perversion, based on the non-recognition by the male . . . that women have no penis.' Certainly, a fetishist enjoys being constrained rather as is a penis in a condom. In addition to body suits, latex panties and tight head masks, he loves the restraint of gags, handcuffs, thumbscrews, strait-jackets, leg-irons and, above all, chastity belts for both sexes. He finds restricted breathing exciting, as the Victorians did, so tight clothing and inflatable mouth gags are important elements in the fantasy.

North describes an outfit made in Germany and 'much in demand by men'. It consists of 'thick rubber skin-tight pants with an opening in the crotch in the form of a hole with its mouth made of a thick rubber ring; the penis is put through this ring (although it is quite hard and requires some effort to stretch it sufficiently) and protrudes with the ring clamped tightly about its root . . . ' The outfit puts modern man in a direct line with his fifteenth-century counterpart in his codpiece. It makes the clubber's genteel S&M leather jacket with non-functional zips and dinky little chains seem very bland. The world of the true fetishist is still a clouded one for most people, who know of its dress only through fashion designers' sanitised borrowings from the uniform of pain. Despite considerable marketing efforts, rubber as a fashion material has not yet caught on in the way that leather has. As a 'sleaze' material it has followers but they are a small element in fashion, and its main appeal remains limited to those who find it sexually exciting.

No such constraints affect leather. It is now worn by people of all ages and classes. From its early associations with blue-collar workers and the 'bad boy' image of James Dean and Marlon Brando, the black leather jacket has been well and truly tamed. It has come through Hell's Angels, who spattered it with graffiti chosen to alienate middle-class sensibilities, via Johnny Rotten and Sid Vicious, who used it as a badge of working-class anarchy, and has even survived the catwalks of Milan where it was paraded by Versace and Ferre as part of the exotic world of high fashion glamour.

Animal skin has always had power over humans. Primitive peoples believed that by donning the pelt of a slain predator such as a lion man inherited its strength and skill as a killer. Kings and the great men who surround them have always used fur as a symbol of their magnificence, in order that they might be viewed by the little people with the same awe with which they would gaze at the lion, tiger, leopard or bear were it alive. But fur was more than a symbol of temporal arrogance and strength. Its close association with death – the tearing claw, the bloodstained tooth – gave it a considerable erotic charge. Sex as a struggle for power is as old as men and women; the fight for dominance is part of even the most humdrum liaison. If it is fought on a leopard-skin rug, it takes the participants right back to cave-age man. The woman in a fur coat has for many men this same primitive association. Magnificent in her borrowed skin, she betokens sex and power, to be overcome but also to overwhelm in her turn. Victor, as well as victim, she produces the same feeling in men that her animal counterpart used to. She has taken on the power, strength and terror of the living creature and she has done more. Fur is, after all, hair – a powerful erotic stimulant in itself. The sensuality of fur is the same as the sexuality of human hair. It does not just remind us of the magnificent mane of the king of beasts – or of the magnificent manes worn by many modern men and women. Vibrant hair is a prerequisite of the sexuality of youth, untamed and untrammelled. It links us with the wild animal, ready to take what it needs, without conscience and without fear. There is a violence in fur as there is in hair, but more: the sexuality of fur links with the hair that protects and highlights the most secret parts of our anatomy. No wonder it has such an arousing effect.

The sensual joy of fur has been besmirched by the cruelty and ruthlessness of the trappers and traders who have decimated the world's stock of big cats. 'Nice' women are not expected to wear fur – and risk verbal and physical attack if they dare do so. But the desire is too strong to be denied. As the trade in fake fur shows, many women still want to assume the power and strength of the animal and do so by wearing a replica as near to the real thing as modern technology can produce. They think that they thus achieve the power without the gore and their consciences are clear. But women who wear fake fur meant to be taken as genuine are as guilty in many ways as those who wear the real thing. They want the sexual frisson bestowed by an animal skin, and it is merely society's disapproval that makes cowards of them. It is understandable that it does. The disapproval is not only violently expressed; it is also frequently dishonest. Behind the façade of care for endangered species lurks the *real* horror and fear. The sexuality that women assume in a big cat's fur seems to exemplify the woman as sexual predator, available only to the strongest and yet, like the animal in the wild, a prey to the superior power of man the hunter. With such complicated semiotics, a fur coat arouses fear and loathing, lust and desire as no other garment can.

Black leather shares some of the same power, despite its more humdrum source. Its overriding appeal comes from its 'butch' image, attractive to men and women alike. Earlier this century, it was the symbol of brutality: Gestapo storm-troopers and Fascist police wore it not just for protection but also for projection. It was meant to instil fear. When it was taken up by bikers in the sixties, it was again not merely for its protective quality; the memory of earlier connotations of super-machismo brutality was an equally powerful factor. Riding a motorbike has a particular appeal for a certain sort of man. He obtains a double pleasure from the machine that throbs between his legs. On the one hand, he can imagine it as a magnificent extension of his virility, on the other as the devil bitch that can only be tamed by that virility. Either way, like the storm-troopers and secret police of the thirties, leather appeals to the sort of man who has never been quite sure of his masculinity and needs a visible proof to clothe it – and to disguise its inadequacies.

This is what links the ordinary man with the rubber fetishist; both feel a heightened sexual awareness when wearing their chosen materials. But women also like to wear leather – and black leather in particular. What effects does it have on them? The fashionable theory is that when the post-feminist woman wears black leather she is revelling in her new status as imitation man, sharing his power, freedom of decision and control over life. If she is, then she is under an illusion. It would take more than black leather to threaten man's control over those areas. No, women who wear black leather do so because they subconsciously seek a substitute for fur. The power they obtain from black leather is the power they once drew from the ocelot's pelt. In this they are no different from men, who, from Nazis to modern bike freaks, have made black leather a surrogate chieftain's animal skin. Even the most wimpish man feels himself a little nearer to mastery of the universe when he dons his leather jacket. His puny masculinity swells within his protective carapace, which acts on him like the Trojan's leather shield, making him feel strong, courageous and masterful. Exactly like a wild animal, he uses his pelt to intimidate his fellow males whilst attracting the females to his overt masculinity.

No wonder the genteel and well bred – no slouches when it comes to the significance of dress – have always been nervous of black leather. Even today, ladies in the shires eschew it as vulgar, working class, tarty – they have many words to show their repugnance, but they rarely voice their real objection. Leather is raunchy. That is its true attraction, and their cause for nervousness. Suede is considered much more suitable and well bred. It is nothing more than leather with no balls, but that, of course, is how the genteel like all aspects of life, be it their music, art, literature or fashion.

They are the people who still believe in the Victorian smoke screen of 'modesty', of not embarrassing one's fellows by anything approximating display – be it emotional or sartorial – and who have damned clothing to a hundred years of stiff upper lip. They are the ones who approved of the skirt to obliterate the seat of female charms. A cursory glance at Victorian female fashion reveals how greatly anal fixation had taken hold of society. The hold it still remarkably strong today. The female bottom has appealed to the British male quite as much as the male bottom. So much so, indeed, that in both cases it has been considered a dangerous incendiary and must, for the sake of human decency, be kept obscured and covered. The one thing we can guarantee would not amuse Queen Victoria were she to pop in to modern London would be the blatant display of buttocks which can be seen on any street, at any time. Not since fifteenth-century Italy have male bums been so exposed – and even then they were a source of great irritation to the authorities who believed that, along with the long and frequently dyed hair affected by young men, they were a major cause of the increasing incidence of buggery. *Plus ça change* . . .

It is because the bottom – male or female – is an instant catalyst for sexual desires that the Victorians would be so uneasy about today's jeans and sweatshirt uniform of the young. The front view would not distress them unduly, but the back view would have them crying out against the breakdown of public decency. And that is just male dress. To see a woman in jeans would truly horrify them. It is not merely that female legs were always shrouded in voluminous skirts. As their bustles, drawn-back skirts and trains show, the Victorians loved bottoms. But they disguised their love under layers of horse hair and padding so that the anatomy of the buttocks was hidden and no longer had the same shape clothed that it had unclothed. Possibly influenced by exciting artists' representations of the Hottentot woman and her awe-inspiring bum, they built it up and out until they had buried its natural contours, just as the Edwardians did with the breasts to create the splendidly named mono-bosom.

Like the corset which, to the Victorians, was 'the fundamental basis of grace', the bustle brought pleasure as well as discomfort. Victorian women understood the erotic charge of a bustle twitching from side to side as they walked, but they were secure in the knowledge that it also gave their appearance a monumentality and their walk a dignity that protected them. Few men would dare to make a sexual advance to a woman so magnificently clad. It was one of many examples of women using clothes to further their coquetry without compromising themselves sexually. That is why they would be appalled at what they would see as the wantonness of two sharply defined and clearly delineated female buttocks outlined in skin-tight ski-pants, leggings or jeans. Such crude sexuality would not, for them, be consistent with the control for which their dress was an essential tool.

Coquetry, allure, even lust, were well-springs of dressing in centuries before this one. Sex, the blatant exploitation of bodies, was not. As the near-nude woman has become the Western norm in the late twentieth century, she has distanced herself from her heavily clothed predecessor. The modern woman's appearance has more in common with that of men than of women from the past. Women finally have sufficient social power to dress as they please and it is no coincidence that they increasingly choose to dress as do men. Their motive has nothing to do with practicality or comfort, even though some have convinced themselves that this is the case. It is hard to argue with Gill's assertion that 'women's dress is more befitting to human dignity than any man's dress . . . because it still retains the general notion of robes' – although, of course, he was referring not to miniskirts but to full, voluminous folds. Women wear the shapes of men's dress because, by doing so, they are psychologically assuming his power along with his trousers. As Polonius said, 'The apparel oft proclaims the man,' and the more masculine a woman's dress seems, the less vulnerable she feels in her sexuality.

Modern women have no time for coquetry: the artful flirtation for compliments. They reject it as unworthy of a sex that is to be taken seriously. They know that a 'sweet disorder', a flowing amorphousness and imprecision in their dress can be alluring, but they are also aware of the basic nuts and bolts of modern life. They realise that the safest protection for their sex is to project it – well-defined outlines and all – as blatantly as do men. I love to see the girl-woman in her jeans, leather jacket and Dr Marten's because she is deliberately not dressing herself as a dish fit for a man, as her predecessors felt they must. She is saying, 'My sexuality is as powerful and as sacrosanct as yours.' With any luck, both halves of the statement will be true before the next century is too old.

The possibility is a real one because her equivalent, the boy-man, vulnerable as well as tough, has finally found the courage to look deeply at the well-springs of his masculinity, and he has seen how rotten were the premises on which his father wanted to base the world. These premises brought the attitudes that have held in check women and the young of all classes; that produced the belief in sexual and class superiority – and their corollary, inferiority; that created the male boss figure, swollen with ill-founded ideas of his right to rule and control the lives and thoughts of others – the man D.H. Lawrence demolished so vituperatively in his poem, 'How beastly the bourgeois is':

How beastly the bourgeois is
especially the male of the species –

Presentable, eminently presentable –
shall I make you a present of him?

Isn't he handsome? Isn't he healthy? Isn't he a fine specimen?
doesn't he look the fresh, clean Englishman, outside?
Isn't it god's own image? tramping his thirty miles a day
after partridges, or a little rubber ball?
wouldn't you like to be like that, well off, and quite the thing?

Oh, but wait!
Let him meet a new emotion, let him be faced with another man's need,
let him come home to a bit of moral difficulty, let life face him with a new demand on his understanding
and then watch him go soggy, like a wet meringue.

Watch him turn into a mess, either a fool or a bully.

Touch him, and you'll find he's all gone inside
just like an old mushroom, all wormy inside, and hollow
under a smooth skin and an upright appearance.

How beastly the bourgeois is!

Where did this preposterous creature come from? How did he develop into such a very unsatisfactory 'other half' of the human equation?

The Great Masculine Betrayal

Men create myths in order to protect themselves from the logic of female scrutiny and one of these myths concerns modern masculine dress. It runs roughly along the following lines: at the end of the eighteenth century, we are told, men found better and more important things to do with their time than devote any thought to their appearance. *The Hermit in London*, published in 1819, berated as coxcombs those men who felt that fashion was worthy of attention 'by any man beyond a tailor's cutter-out, a man-milliner, or a monkey hairdresser'. Interest in dress, henceforth, was to be a feminine preoccupation, outside the range of a rational man's concerns. Whereas excessive interest in one's appearance had traditionally been considered the proof positive of vanity and empty-headedness, now *any* interest in dress was thought to betoken a chink of feminine weakness in the masculine mind. Such is the male rationalisation – but the story does not stand up.

How did such a nonsensical idea come about? To find this out, it is necessary to look briefly at certain aspects of eighteenth-century life and to examine what fashion actually meant at that time.

Colley Cibber's oft-quoted remark 'As good be out of the world as out of the fashion,' referred not merely to dress. Like Dr Johnson's frequently quoted comment that a man who is tired of London is tired of life, it referred to the fashionable life – the world of routs, visits to Vauxhall and Ranelagh, being seen at the play, and dining with and gossiping about one's friends. In the early decades of the eighteenth century this seemed a very satisfactory way of passing the time for gentlemen of leisure – what would now be called the idle rich – and there were plenty of them about. However, excess began to cloy. To the more intelligent members of society, London and its fashionable round became boringly repetitive, little more than an excuse for dressing up, with life reduced to the level of a charade.

That fashionable London life appealed less to men and women of the upper classes as the eighteenth century progressed is manifest in the increasing time and thought they devoted to their country acres. Endless portraits of patricians surrounded by the evidence of the wealth that could only be bestowed by ownership of vast tracts of land indicate that the aristocracy sensed that what gave it superiority over the increasingly powerful middle class was the security of green acres. Portraits showing aristocrats surrounded by the wealth and power of land, in the style of *Mr and Mrs Andrews* by Gainsborough, became increasingly popular. The middle class – the lawyers, doctors, merchants and shipowners – could be portrayed in an urban setting; what gave the upper classes their cachet was the rural setting that they alone commanded and the rural clothes that went along with their exclusive way of life.

The city clothes of the aristocrat had usually been fancy. Reflecting the fact that many of life's pleasures in London were enjoyed indoors, or in such artificial outdoor surroundings as Ranelagh and Vauxhall, the emphasis was on exotic and even delicate fabrics of a kind unfitted for exposure to the harsher realities of the open-air climate. But these fabrics – silks elaborately embroidered, velvets braided with gold, lace delicately worked by hand – were not suitable for the outdoor country life that the landed classes increasingly relied on as their one impregnable power-base.

Plain spun and sensibly shod, the newly converted country gentleman turned his back on the more decorative aspects of dress, which were the province of the exquisite urbanite. Because the gentleman was still perceived as the fount of all taste, mainstream male dress, including that of the upwardly mobile middle-class male, became simpler. Elborately fashionable wear held less and less appeal. Eventually it was worn only by the most dedicated urban followers of fashion – the fops and the effeminates who gave full range to their metropolitan urges and, like French courtiers, viewed rural life as a horrid black chasm from which there could be no return.

When fashion moves on and leaves behind those who wish to stand still, it presents them with a problem. In order to enjoy and sustain the illusion that they are at the cutting edge of style, and not marooned in the past, they must dedicate increasing amounts of time to their appearance and must exaggerate those characteristics of the fashion that were originally so attractive to them. In our own times we have only to look at what happened to faded jeans. As they became so thin that they split, they made a fashionable statement with a universal appeal to the young. When fashion moved on to stone-washed jeans, robust and practical, those who loved split jeans slashed their new ones in order to re-create the look they loved. Similarly, when they lost their power to shock and began to look like old-fashioned waifs, punks exaggerated their make-up and hairstyles rather than shift their philosophical stance and become fashionable by following the lines of hip hop and acid house.

Stuck in the amber of their lack of imagination, the one-time leaders of eighteenth-century fashion became increasingly ridiculous and out of touch in their dress. Their appearance finally received the *coup de grâce* from playwrights and satirists who laughed them out of existence by contrasting their foppish dress with the plainer styles of the now truly fashionable and portrayed them as increasingly feminine, if not effeminate. It was the first seed of what J.C. Flügel was to call The Great Masculine Renunciation, when 'men gave up their right to all the brighter, gayer, more elaborate and more varied forms of ornamentation'.

Flügel considered that men gave up elaborate dress which proclaimed social distinctions and differences in wealth because the French Revolution had made the aristocracy cagey about endangering their lives as well as their social positions by flaunting such distinctions.

In fact, the Great Masculine Renunciation came before the French Revolution. It was not primarily a renunciation of bright clothing. It was a renunciation of a way of life. Pragmatism and practicality demanded a change of style, not a rejection of elegance. Riding coats and breeches were cut with the same precision as court velvets; a country gentleman's boots were as perfectly shaped as urban shoes. The glamour of quality had taken over from the headiness of excess; the sophistication of simplicity replaced glitter that now seemed vulgar. The renunciation of decorative dress was a consequence, not a cause, of the new attitude. The new rural uniform was the aristocrat's preferred day wear although, for evening wear, male dress continued for a while to retain much of its earlier extravagance.

A parallel process of adjustment and rationalisation took place in women's dress in the first decade of the twentieth century. Impractical wear was abandoned for the daytime, but for evening wear decorative extravagance remained – as it does still. A modern woman's ball gown is frequently no more practical than the hoops and crinolines of the past, but her day clothes would seem outrageously masculine in their practicality and plainness to women of the eighteenth or nineteenth centuries. Indeed, they would find modern day wear unbelievable in its simplicity, quite apart from the amount of the body that it exposes.

By the beginning of the nineteenth century, men who still dressed in too fanciful a style were considered more feminine in their approach than most women. From this it was a small step to branding them as homosexuals, which possibly many of them were. In any event, their lasting effect was to tar for ever with this brush any man who dressed imaginatively. Even today the suspicion holds. Despite Carlyle's belief that 'The first spiritual want of a barbarous man is Decoration,' we still think that the decorative urge, in all males of the species except the very young, is unmanly. The belief persists in stubborn defiance of the evidence to the contrary provided by soldiers' ceremonial dress, which is nothing if not flamboyantly decorative, though the wearers of it are manly – and frequently barbarous – beyond dispute.

How did the upper-class male – the ruling figure – go from fop through dandy to mid-Victorian paterfamilias in less than a hundred years? His sartorial downfall, initiated by himself, was largely brought about by the middle classes and their increasing stranglehold on morality and propriety. As the nineteenth century progressed, they altered social attitudes to such an extent that lingering eighteenth-century dualism in male dress – practical day, decorative night – gradually changed to universal and uniform plainness.

There have been many explanations for this change, more a betrayal than a simple renunciation. All contain at least a grain of truth. Many factors contributed to it. Clearly, the rapid growth of urban conurbations with their attendant grime belching out of factory chimneys twenty-four hours per day made light, delicate or rich fabrics impractical – Septimus Piesse complained in *The Art of Perfumery* in 1862 of the sulphurous atmosphere of cities 'charged with the products of combustion of gas and coal'. The increasingly hallowed work ethic that dominated the middle classes at all levels made decorative clothing seem frivolous and self-indulgent. The belief in sobriety made flashiness seem vulgar. But these are secondary causes. The extravagant peacock was killed by middle-class attitudes to education and sexuality, not by the need for practical clothing. Nineteenth-century male power-dressing (high stiff collars, tight waistcoats and stovepipe hats) was quite definitely not practical but it was sober. As such it reflected a new sense of responsibility towards at least one aspect of nineteenth-century male sexuality.

Homosexuality has generally been frowned upon by the state as a threat to the family and therefore to social stability, and by the Church because it negates procreation, the religious basis for sexuality, and thus devalues marriage. In this respect the eighteenth century was a rare age of tolerance. Upper-class homosexuals and bisexuals were, if not openly accepted, certainly not rejected by their peers. Homosexual indiscretion could be dismissed as an idiosyncratic luxury of the wealthy. A roistering man was permitted his catamite as well as his doxy, provided that his demeanour betrayed no effeminacy. This was the sticking point. Effeminate men alone were the outright targets for disapproval, just as, among sexual acts, only sodomy attracted real opprobrium. In all other matters, if homosexuals were discreet and resorted to molly houses for their pleasure, they were reasonably safe. Found mainly in the Covent Garden area of London, molly houses – virtually male brothels – were institutions unheard of by the majority of the population, but they provided an important safety outlet for homosexual society.

Although many Restoration rakes may have been bisexual, it was only towards the end of the eighteenth century that certain hairstyles, cuts of clothes, attitudes to personal hygiene and decorative jewellery, in conjunction with an extravagantly expressive voice and demeanour, began to be seen as betokening lack of manliness on a level that could cast doubt on a man's sexuality. Intolerance based on dress was not new, but suspicion of sexual proclivities based on styles of dress was.

Growing disapproval of homosexuality (which can be measured by the number of men brought into court during the later years of the eighteenth century) can be seen as a corollary of the developing bureaucratic influence of the middle-class desire for impartial and universal order. Whereas for most of the century organisation of the law had been regional, *ad hoc* and subject to local pressures, by the beginning of the nineteenth century criminality was codified with greater precision; legal administration was imposed more rigidly by centralised administration, and respect for the rule of law had become a tenet of the ruling classes in general.

Aristocratic roisterers were no longer beyond and above the rules of society. Although it was not until 1869 that Karoly Benkert coined the word *homosexualist*, and not until 1885 that Labouchère's amendment to the Criminal Law Amendment Act made private, as well as public, acts of gross indecency between males liable to a penalty of two years in prison 'with or without hard labour', effeminacy of dress – that is, decorative dress of the kind considered perfectly normal in court and aristocratic circles in the early decades of the eighteenth century – had become a dangerous pointer to attitudes increasingly disapproved of and even punished by society. Such a belief was the inevitable result of the idealisation of the family and the sentimentalising of women as wives and mothers, soon to be a major characteristic of the new century.

Was the idealisation and sentimentalising of women – especially mothers – a conscious effort by men to assuage their feelings of guilt over pushing women into a domestic ghetto out of which it would take a hundred years for them to escape, or was it a subconscious and gradual process that was not perceived until too late to undo the damage? Either way, women were effectively entombed in the home as the great Victorian commercial push that would make Great Britain the leader of the world got under way. Men became industrialised but women, apart from the working-class cannon fodder that the manufacturing industries sucked into the emerging urban centres like Manchester, Bradford and Halifax, had no role in the new urban order. As a magazine article put it: 'the peculiar province of Woman is to tend with patient assiduity the bed of sickness; to watch the feeble steps of infancy . . . and bless with their smiles those of their friends who are declining in the vale of tears.'

Having lost their traditional role as helpmates to their men in the running of farms and small country estates, and with rural skills no longer able to be employed, women were now irrelevant in the world outside the home. They were merely the breeders and the keepers of the family hearth. Quite apart from the heady world of commerce and industry, men refused to see a place for women in any sphere of public life. An article on 'the Grievances of Women' summed up the early Victorian male attitudes. 'Picture', it exclaimed in horror, 'an elegant, beautiful woman taking part in the vulgar squabbles of a vestry-room or entering the stormy arena of politics! Where then would be the quiet joys of domestic home?' It was not so much that men did not want to see women in public life as a fear that it might reflect on the comfort of their homes – the nests they returned to hoping for a warm and devoted welcome that would assuage the horrors of the world outside. To make such selfishness palatable it was sugared with the argument that women were too pure a sex to mix in the crude and corrupting world beyond their front doors; 'The opposite sex love, respect and adore women and ever will, so long as they retain that inestimable jewel, Virtue.'

The male's nest was the female's cage but it was also meant to be her toy. However, it could not be guaranteed as a placebo for all, any more than marriage and children could. Far too many nineteenth-century bachelors enjoyed their state too much to change it by marriage, no matter how materially advantageous. And so the universal toy for the Victorian woman debarred from work and not secure in her own 'establishment' became herself. She had her own person as her hobby, to decorate, beautify and distort to her heart's content, with society's full approval – an approval that has lasted to this day. Trapped in enforced decorative idleness, she gave fashion its greatest impetus in history. By encouraging the belief that decorativeness was essentially and exclusively a female prerogative, men not only stunted the mental growth of women; they also stunted their own emotional growth to such an extent that, even now, they lag behind women in the sensitivity and sensibility essential for a balanced society. Softness, gentleness and understanding are not God-given feminine traits. They are only made to seem so because men kicked them out of their lives at the crucial moment when modern approaches to education were being codified.

As John Stuart Mill pointed out, in *The Subjugation of Women*, in 1869, 'What is called the nature of Women is an eminently artificial thing – the result of forced repression in some directions, unnatural stimulation in others . . . The masters of women wanted more than simple obedience, and they turned the whole force of education to effect their purpose . . . And this great means of influence over the minds of women having been acquired, an instinct of selfishness made men avail themselves of it to the utmost as a means of holding women in subjection, by representing to them meekness, submissiveness, and resignation of all individual will into the hands of a man, as an essential part of sexual attractiveness . . . '

The type of education suitable for the 'gentle sex' was an old sore that had disturbed forward-looking men and troubled intellectual women for generations. As early as 1688, François de Salignac de la Mothe-Fénelon had suggested that men must keep women's minds 'within the usual limits, and let them understand that the modesty of their sex ought to shrink from science with almost as much delicacy as from vice'. Lady Mary Wortley Montagu, writing to her daughter in 1752, explained how ill at ease an educated woman made men feel: 'We are educated in the grossest ignorance, and no art omitted to stifle our natural reason. If some few get above their nurses' instructions, our knowledge must rest concealed and be as useless to the world as gold in the mine . . . ' In 1791, Mary Wollstonecraft took up the theme in her *Vindication of the Rights of Women* when she pointed out that 'women are systematically degraded by receiving the trivial attentions which men think it manly to pay to the sex, when, in fact, they are insultingly supporting their own superiority . . . ' Her frustration was echoed by Mary Berry, writing in 1806: 'When you men are sent to college we are left . . . to positive idleness, without any object, end or aim to encourage any one employment of our mind more than another . . . '

The male equation was a simple one. It was the propaganda of a sex in charge, but running scared that it might not remain so without resorting to drastic repression of the female intellect. Women had to be made to look inwards and see the domestic world as the limit of their ambitions and hopes. Further, they had to be made as obsessed with their appearance as men were with power. To point the contrast in the sexes, clothes

ATTENTION SEEKING

Male erogenous zones are as important as female ones, with the difference that, until recently, men, not women, decided what they would be. In order to hide their greatest preoccupation and source of insecurity (the size and performance of the male member) they invented the myth that the true erogenous zone for women is the man's head and the brain inside it. In the late middle ages, men chose to show their social superiority by drawing attention to the male genital area. Even in the civilised late twentieth century, our term of praise for a man's skill, courage and achievement is that he has balls. Secondary but not unimportant in the male mind is the attraction of his bottom. Whereas for most of history the cleavage of the female derrière has been covered and disguised to such an extent that it has largely been a mono-bum, with all contours muffled in clothing, the male has consistently flaunted the shape of his rear as a symbol of his power and strength. Michael Clark shocked the ballet-loving public not so much because they did not wish to see a well defined naked bum, but because, by exposing his, he commited an artistic faux pas.

MORNING   NOON   NIGHT

FORM AND FINESSE

There is no point in being fashionable if it is easy for others to copy you. The less practical clothing is, the more prestigious and the more suggestive of money it will be. If your trousers are so tight that it is not possible to bend down and poke the fire, then you must employ someone in less constricting dress to do so for you. Again, if you choose to wear white and pale shades, you are letting it be known that you do not have to do anything that might make you dirty. You pay others to do those things for you. Tissot's elegant couple out for the evening are perfect exemplars of the attitude. The Regency dandies of 1826, dressed morning noon and night for leisure, are telling society that they also live off the bent backs of others. Although in a cartoon, and therefore presenting an exaggerated idea of reality, these clothes show what might be termed the last glorious sunburst of male coquetry before it sank for ever into the sartorial black night of the nineteenth century. Its concepts of respectability and suitability as exemplified by the boringly unexceptional dress of the bourgeois male were personified to perfection in the domestic rectitude of Victoria's Consort, Prince Albert.

43

FASHIONABLE FIGURES

Eric Gill felt that trousers were a shaming item of clothing that constrained men and gave them an undignified appearance. He argued that the dress of biblical times was more appropriate to the human anatomy. Many women have felt that the skirt was the most constraining item of dress and the twentieth century has seen them adopt trousers or jeans for everyday wear for the first time in history.

In the nineteenth century, women wore constricting skirts in order that they might walk in a lady-like way – that is, with a gait as different as possible from the dominant male stride.

Although the modern model is wearing clothing which might seem inappropriate to modern life, in that its volume and shape are impractical for entry to cars or lifts, incommodious for small flats and offices and too large for swiftness of movement, she can 'walk like a man', confident of her equal status.

THEATRICAL EXTRAVAGANCES

Why did women allow themselves to be shunted into the backwater of history by willingly becoming the over-decorated sex? Although this eighteenth century woman is dressed for a fancy dress ball in a costume originally designed for a theatrical production, her clothes are not far removed from the actual dress of the period. Stiff and heavy skirts, exaggerated sleeves and cumbersome headwear were accepted as the lot of the well-born and wealthy woman. Clearly, these were status clothes of the most blatant kind in an age when modesty was the rule in middle class and artisan circles, and poverty precluded decoration in the lower classes. Was the object of such extravagance to be attractive sexually or was it merely a parade of the power of money? Certainly, the seducer faced with this amount of clothing had to be as persistent as Casanova and as resourceful as Valmont.

But old habits die hard. Even modern couturiers can send down the runway clothes like these by Lacroix and be applauded. Is it natural at the end of the twentieth century to wish to be dressed like a Christmas cracker – and, if it is, why does only one sex appear to crave it?

MAKING A CHOICE

Pop entertainers have been very successful in breaking down barriers of sexuality and destroying mindless taboos. Stars such as Mick Jagger and David Bowie have shown the world that a man is not necessarily turned into a woman by wearing a dress or make-up. However, they spawned a host of followers, on the stage and on the disco floor, for whom the whole point was to look as camp and effeminate as possible. Freddie Mercury of Queen was probably the king of them all, managing to look as magnificent in drag as he looked butch in vest and jeans.

Destroying sexual stereotypes does not mean breaking down sexual differences. In this century, women have not become lesbians because they wear trousers, and no sane person would make the preposterous assumption that they would. However, when the male attempts a similar course it is usually assumed he is gay. Male sexuality is insecure whilst women's is confident, because for generations men have embraced the belief that their power and might are a result of their masculinity rather than their ability, aptitude or personality.

RUFFLED AND RIPPED

The decorative urge is not an exclusively female characteristic, as we have been led to believe. It has visited men throughout history and at all social levels. For an eighteenth century French prince it was important to look magnificently god-like to ensure that his actions were beyond question. For the seventies' punk , it was necessary to show your rejection of the values of a materialistic society. Both created a remarkably similar effect.

51

were pushed to extremes in the nineteenth century, the century above all others in which the gap between the intellectual, emotional and even moral standards expected of men and women yawned wide. Vanity and triviality were exemplified on the female side by ever-changing and increasingly excessive fashions; rectitude and reliability were shown to be the true lot of men through clothing which changed style as infrequently and surreptitiously as possible.

If an arbitrary decision is made that plainness and sobriety of dress are the prerequisites of the governing sex, and the other sex is encouraged, or even forced, into an obsessive preoccupation with decorative variations in dress, then that sex cannot pose a serious challenge to the hegemony of the governing sex. Further, if the governing sex reserves to itself the form of education it has deemed suitable for governors and does not allow the second sex to benefit from it, then it perpetuates itself as a governing class and condemns the other sex to involvements that are trivial and non-threatening. That is what men did to women in the nineteenth century when they renounced decorative clothing and made it a plaything for the 'ladies'. They placed women on a pedestal, out of the way, to be admired and noticed only when men wished them to be, as decorative, even valuable, artistic acquisitions, but mute and irrelevant in terms of the real, masculine world beyond the dressmaker's establishment. Was it fear or gaucherie that made it happen? As late as 1871, *The Queen* could still write that, 'underneath the conventional surface of politeness is a deep undercurrent of enmity. The strange fight that has long been going on between the sexes about the various professions to which women have laid claim testifies to the truth of this.' Decorative women might be; businesslike they must not be. Men had claimed that world exclusively for themselves when they handed over to women fashion's frivolity.

Not that in renouncing decoration men had renounced style. Taking the countryman's riding coat as the basis of their fashion, they made it part of an elegant, even sophisticated approach to dressing that not only upheld their hierarchical right to command, but also perpetuated their right to dress in a way that was overtly sexual. With the new century, male clothes became a contrast of light and dark: blue, black and bottle green for coats, and cream, buff and white for breeches and, later, trousers. The colour balance is not without significance. Regency and early Victorian breeches were worn very tight, as pantaloons and breeches had been in the previous century. They outlined the legs and the genitals in a calculated and provocative way. Because they were in pale colours they drew attention to male attributes in a way that, had jackets been light-coloured and pantaloons dark, would not have happened. Although we do not find any reference to it in Jane Austen, women were perfectly aware of what men's dress was about, as the famous hatter, Lloyd, in a treatise on his different styles for customers in 1819, makes clear when he describes, with heavy innuendo, a hat known as a 'Bit of Blood' as being of value to 'elderly gentlemen in pursuit of young wives, who nine times out of ten decide on the choice of a man from the *cock* – of his hat . . . '

Just as the shoulders and breasts of women have throughout history been highlighted as signifiers of sexuality, so inevitably have the genitals of the male. Whereas the codpiece drew attention to what *might* be available, the early nineteenth century breeches made perfectly clear what *was* available. With such exposure, it does not take much imagination to envisage what would be revealed if a Regency buck were sexually aroused in public whilst wearing such clothes. It was an embarrassment that might well have been avoided – or at least visually diminished – had the colour balance been reversed. Men knew perfectly well how provocative they looked; they clearly wished it so and were prepared to suffer for the right effect, even as women did. *Chamber's Edinburgh Review* of 1850 recalls the fashionable man of the earlier part of the century as wearing bucksins so tight that they stopped the flow of blood 'in a downward direction' so that it 'mounted upward, made his neck and his face swell and his eyes protrude, and turned his cheeks as red as the gills of a fish'.

If men did not renounce style, neither did they entirely renounce decoration. Provided that it was in an 'all boys together' situation, decorative clothing was not always considered effeminate in the nineteenth century. Such a situation existed in the military. As the civilian man's clothes became increasingly sober, uniforms grew more exotically provocative. Stylised and decorative, they allowed the Victorian male to give full vent to his pent-up need to look magnificent, arrogant and, above all, sexually powerful. Breeches grew tighter as Hussars, Dragoons and Foot regiments vied to outdo each other in dash and panache. Crimson, white, lavender, indigo and forest green were all used for pantaloons and trousers; scarlet and blue tunics, faced with contrasting colours at collar and cuff, were liberally sparkled with gold. Headgear of swans' feathers, fur, gold and silver was beplumed, crested and finialled with an extravagance that would have kept the most demanding Ruritanian princeling happy. Officers and men swaggered in their peacockery, only too aware of the effects their magnificently decorative uniforms were having on their female admirers. And they got away with it because it was a universally acknowledged truth that to inspire confidence and fear (the prerequisites of the military) a man *must* swagger and he best does so in clothes that are flamboyant. The swagger denotes the magnificence of masculinity; it is a sexual thing every bit as much to do with the bed as the battlefield. A superb and theatrical uniform convinces that the soldier can be victorious in both.

Why didn't this magnificent sexual confidence spill over into civilian life? For the answer we must look at the effect of the new education on the nineteenth-century male and the way it coloured how he saw himself *and* women.

The huge increase in the numbers of the urban middle classes brought a corresponding need for a gentleman's education for them. The nineteenth century was the great century of the public school. The frequently slipshod aristocratic education of the past had to be tamed and institutionalised for the vastly increased numbers demanding an education suitable for leaders, and even heroes, of the empire that was only just beginning to be stolen from the world. The tone was set by the formidable Dr Arnold, headmaster of Rugby from 1827 to 1842. His influence on the ethics of the new education was considerable – the staffroom at Rugby was like a hothouse, bringing on young masters who eventually burst into bloom as headmasters themselves, ready to carry on the Arnold ethic. As Mark Girouard has said in *The Return to Camelot*, his absorbing study of Victorian male attitudes, 'In the eighteenth century schoolmasters had confined themselves to teaching and beating boys: Arnold tried to make them good as well.' By doing so, he gave the young Victorian male not only a conscience but also a sense of guilt.

Victorian public schools were hotbeds of unnaturally heightened feeling. As Disraeli wrote in 1844, 'At school, friendship is a passion; it entrances the being; it tears the soul. All loves of afterlife can never bring its rapture . . .' J.A. Symonds, writing of Harrow in the 1850s, recalled that one 'could not avoid seeing acts of onanism, mutual masturbation, the sport of naked boys in bed together'. Wrenched away from their mothers and homes, placed in the over-heated, enclosed world of adolescent boyhood, it is not surprising that two things developed from the public-school experience which permanently affected the male psyche. Love of school as surrogate home became so strong that loyalty to school house transcended devotion to family. With it came the guilt caused by the rejection of emotional ties with the mother and identification with an entirely male world. It led to a morbid fear of adult homosexuality alongside an over-compensatory treatment of women. As Mrs Lynn Linton wrote in *The Girl of the Period* in 1867, recalling her youth: 'women of a certain class were absolutely secure from insult, because the education of their brothers, as of our fathers, included that kind of chivalrous respect for the weaker sex which was then regarded as inseparable from true gentlehood and real civilisation.' Victorian men made their females into strange creatures to be revered and respected as half-goddess and half-angel – provided that they stayed firmly in their place, in charge of drawing room or nursery and, when released, walked metaphorically one step behind their master.

In dress, the lasting result of the public-school experience was to consolidate the rejection of any form of clothing that could have connotations of femininity or originality. As the century progressed, sombre richness was all that was permitted alongside the elegant simplicity of the socially assured male. It can be argued that the stiff white collar, dark frock coat and impeccably cut trousers of the wealthy Victorian reached an apogee of sophistication, subsequently lost, brilliantly delineated by Dickens in 'Dombey and Son' when he describes Dombey senior as 'one of those close-shaved, close-cut, moneyed gentlemen who are glossy and crisp like new bank notes, and who seem to be artificially braced and tightened as by the stimulating action of golden showerbaths.'

Fear of the taint of homosexuality honed everything down to a streamlined silhouette, uninterrupted by extraneous detail, and always decorous, unchallenging and safely unremarkable. Conversely, the men so dressed encouraged their women to dress with an unprecedented decorative excess. It was almost as though simplicity and clutter had respectively become shorthand for masculinity and femininity. No well-bred male could draw attention to himself by originality in dress, unless he inhabited the twilit world of artist and poet, and no middle-class woman could afford not to have the latest frills and furbelows, unless deeply influenced by the new Nonconformity.

Women had been hijacked, their lives shunted off the main line, but the majority of middle- and upper-class wives appeared perfectly happy with the situation. Provided they could silence their intellects and quell their independence of thought, there were many compensations to be found in well-to-do society. They frequently had considerable freedom within society's constraints – that is, the constraints of 'good form' set up by men but eagerly multiplied and codified by women themselves in order to break the ennui of having very little except trivialities to fill their days. At all times it was assumed that they would follow Lord Lyttelton's advice to a lady: 'Seek to be good, but aim not to be great.'

The Victorian novelists such as George Eliot and Mrs Gaskell give us a good, and probably accurate, idea of the lives of comfortably middle-class women at this time. If they were 'well-married', their style of life could be gratifyingly opulent. Dragooned into becoming the shopping sex, most of them contrived to enjoy it, despite criticism of the very role they were encouraged to play. *The Times* of 1873 thundered, 'It is lamentable that the gentler sex have a good deal to do with the ruinous extravagance which introduces all the vices and ruins all the virtues; they dress at a rate far beyond their incomes; they are such creatures of rivalry and display that they cannot help feeling a sort of triumph over those who are less fortunate.' Quite apart from the joys of shopping, well-off women had other compensations. They ate well, they drank well. Victorian and Edwardian women owed much of their monumentality of figure to the considerable quantities of fortified sweet wines and alcoholic cordials they imbibed daily

– Robert Louis Stevenson wrote in *Virginibus Puerisque* of women 'who have a taste for brandy and no heart . . .' and a newspaper report of 1887 pointed out that 'intemperance exists to a frightful extent among educated women.' But, above all, as if to compensate for their husbands' sartorial self-denial, they adored decorative detail.

And men adored them for it. Metaphorically snatched from the female womb in order to be schooled, they spent a lifetime feeling bereft, riven by guilt or in awe of women. They lived a proxy decorative life through their wives – encouraging and applauding each new extravagance of female fashion, although dismissing it with sneering contempt in the masculine safety of their clubs. It was no accident that it was in late Victorian times that *Punch* became so searingly satirical about the excesses of feminine fashion, although it was read just as avidly in the drawing room as in the club. For all the laughter, youthful deprivation of maternal comfort and sisterly companionship ensured that, despite the image of Victorian England as sternly masculine, most men were dizzy with joy at the increasingly impractical and varied feminine fashions – especially as developments such as the crinoline and the bustle made any advance in a man's world as difficult literally as it was metaphorically or idealistically.

Flick through an illustrated book of Victorian fashions and you are left wondering where on earth they all came from – and indeed why. To understand, it is necessary to return to the public-school system. The code of chivalry it inculcated was based on honour – the honour of self-effacement. The English gentleman was expected to sacrifice his own interests for the good of the country and the glory of its female monarch, Victoria. Men so trained would be above the sordid cut and thrust of the daily fight for supremacy. But human nature meant that the ideal was rarely achieved. Instead men who were ambitious – and the Victorian male was highly competitive – learned to disguise this less desirable element in their characters so that the overtly ambitious were condemned as bounders, not quite gentlemen. It was a cunning approach that left women conveniently exposed as the competitive, ambitious sex, vying to outshine each other for their husbands' gratification, using fashion as their medium.

Fashion thrives on competition. The ornamental urge cannot stand still. Fashion competition is about moving from one form of fashion conformity to another. Nowhere was this better understood than in the drawing rooms of Victorian England, through which, as Girouard says, 'queenly ladies, noble by nature . . . as good as they were beautiful and as artistic as they were good' sailed 'in a distinctive atmosphere of love, worship and deference' – buoyed up, he might have added, by the power of their personal presence. Whereas a man, as Thomas Hughes's immensely influential *Tom Brown's Schooldays* had Squire Brown observe, must 'turn out a brave, helpful, truth-telling Englishman, and a gentleman', a woman had to turn out modest, beautiful and permanently maidenly, worthy of the honour and protection afforded her by the chivalrous male. But above all she must be decorative – aggressively, competitively so.

In the eighteenth century, when fashion was predominantly an upper-class preoccupation, both sexes enjoyed its rhythm and change. The nineteenth century saw fashion increasingly confined to the female sex. It also became a bourgeois occupation. The competition that drove fashion change had itself become an element in the competition of class power. In the eighteenth century, rivalry to be the first with something new and original had only really existed within the upper classes, with the middle classes rivalling each other in their aping of the fashions already set by their 'betters'. Although all men were clearly not equal, all gentlemen – and their ladies – were and it was their prerogative to set the style. Fashion became political in the nineteenth century when the battle for social power was joined between the upper and middle classes. The competition that drove fashion change had itself become an element in the struggle for that power.

Like countermarching armies, the sexes swept off in different directions. The result was that, over the century, male dress became increasingly standardised as female dress grew more varied. The concept of obsolescence, vital to fashion change, barely existed in men's clothing in that a man could wear clothes clearly old-fashioned without causing mirth, whereas if a woman were out of fashion, the fact would cause not just mirth but shame. It was a step forward from the old eighteenth-century joke about the country yokel coming to town feeling proud in what were fashionable clothes years earlier and causing his town relations embarrassment because he did not know that fashion had moved on. This time the shame in such a situation would not be nearly so bad for the squire as for his lady. Women were expected to know and respond to fashion change. It was mandatory to do so. For men, clearly acknowledged as the superior sex, it was unnecessary.

The Victorian male was a collector of the most rapacious and avid kind. As the century moved forward he collected countries and whole continents for the Queen. Once they were safely under the British flag, he then collected their flora and fauna in an orgy of caging, killing, stuffing, mounting and pressing. He collected their people and made them soldiers, workers and minor civil servants to the Queen. He denuded their countries for her and her British subjects. The Empire was one huge collection amassed by the skill and ruthlessness of the British middle-class male, whose reasons were not merely economic. By creating such a superb collection of possessions, he was subconsciously aping the upper classes who had done the same with art and sculpture in the previous century. Their horizons had been modest enough: their hunting ground was Europe; their quarry, a few great pictures; their object, to demonstrate cultural and educational superiority. The Victorian middle-class collectors were much more ambitious. They took on the world. They wished to control and possess the products of all known continents.

Victorian England was characterised by the founding of great museums and art galleries. What is the point of collecting, if you cannot display your possessions? But collecting was not confined to inanimate objects. The period saw the creation of the great moving, breathing collections exhibited in the newly created zoos, the exotic plant gardens and arboretums. The pleasures to be gained from these collections were mainly appreciated by the middle classes. What interest could a zoo hold for an aristocrat whose father's pleasure had been to watch the lunatics in Bedlam, and who already had gardens and possessions enough? How could the working classes appreciate such mass acquisitiveness when, by contrast, they had nothing?

Taking his lead from Prince Albert, the middle-class male's greatest collection was his family. The idea that Victorian families were large because of fear of high child mortality and unreliable birth-control methods is not wrong, but it does not take into consideration the psychological state of the Victorian middle class male. He was a collector and a possessor. He was prodigal. He was excited by the teeming world of nature *and* the vast resources of the new industrial processes. He thought big, because the world he had uncovered made him feel small. Its vastness, after Darwin's revelation that his ancestor was a 'hairy quadruped', made the Victorian middle-class male feel as biologically insignificant as his aristocratic neighbour made him feel socially inferior. However, in his domestic situation he could right the balance. He could be as fertile not only as even the most prodigal of eighteenth-century grandees but as nature herself. No mean-spirited 'one boy, one girl, basta!' approach for him. As monarch of all he surveyed around his family hearth, the Victorian male emulated in his sexual prodigality the excesses of the two greatest discoveries of the age: nature and empire.

Victorian England was overwhelmed by both. The beauties, glories and terrors of nature were a constant, frequently unwelcome, reminder that man was puny. To counteract such thoughts, it had to be conquered. The twin paths to overcoming the awesomeness of nature were voyages of discovery, from which the traveller returned burdened down with the captured proofs of his superiority, and the development of inventions to subdue nature's power – to control it in the way the Victorian male wished to control everything. Canning had boasted that he called the New World into existence to redress the balance of the Old. It was a boast that Victorian males understood: the Empire was essentially a middle-class, bourgeois achievement, fit attribute for a middle-class country and a bourgeois queen. The Victorian middle-class home, from Windsor Castle down, was a domestic zoo, a collector's cage into which were popped the finest specimens that reflected most impressively the skills of the collector. Like nature and empire, it had to teem with offspring. The Victorian male had to be seen as being every bit as fertile as the bison or the Hottentot. And just as a tiger was prized for the magnificence of its pelt, so the female specimens in the domestic zoo had to be magnificently clothed. Just because the Victorian male dressed plainly – as befitted the man of action and the hunter – was no reason for his prime specimens to do the same.

It is no accident that the nineteenth century brought to a high point the art of taxidermy. Victorians wanted things kept under control, presented at their peak. What better way to achieve this than by killing and stuffing them? But, of all their treasures, the specimens of which Victorian men felt most proud were their women. And by cocooning them in the gilded domestic world and encouraging them to preen and posture in their beautiful plumage like so many exotic birds, they effectively stuffed and mounted them as the specimens of their skills and prowess that they undoubtedly felt they were.

Most women loved the preening and the posturing, as, indeed would have men, had they been afforded the chance. The desire to present oneself to the best advantage is not confined to one sex. Women were encouraged to become the preeners and posturers of society by the stimulus of seemingly endless fashion reports and 'intelligences' from Paris. Published in the weekly magazines, with increasingly detailed illustrations, these fed the desire for change in a way as manipulative as it was coercive. As a letter in *The Queen* said in 1862, 'vanity and fashion will have their sway . . .' With such encouragement – even indoctrination – many women found consolation for the emptiness of their lives by becoming dedicated followers of fashion. They submerged their personalities entirely in their dress – in fact, following the lead pointed for them by their men, they used their dress to define their personalities. It is not surprising that Victorians loved musical boxes. They perfectly reflected male attitudes to women. Lift the lid, and a pretty little marionette – little more than a dressed and dancing version of a stuffed animal – pirouettes to a tinkling tune. Her gaze is vacant but her dress is lovely. Most important, when her appearance and tune become boring, the hand that lifted the lid can snap it closed and silence her. The hand was always male, of course.

Valuable insights into Victorian middle- and upper-class worlds can be gained from the novels of Trollope. They show the joys and horrors of Victorian domestic life but, for their Victorian readers, they contained the seeds of future hope for women. Trollope's heroines, from Mrs Proudie to Lady Glencora, had the wit and spirit to play the male game on their own terms. No male could cow Lizzie Eustace. Such women were the fictional precursors of the late Victorian and Edwardian reality, the powerful women who dressed in the latest fashion as a matter of pride, not merely to reflect her husband's worth and position: Lady Waterford, Lady Mount Temple, Lady Marian Alford and their like. Such women would be the decorated victims of no man. It was just such upper-class women, often the wives of men newly ennobled, who unlocked the cage and stepped out into the real world of intellectual freedom. They were followed by the middle-class women who were to demand the very things their men wished to keep to themselves: education, the vote, a public life. They were the first modern women, although their progress was hampered as much by their own as by the opposite sex. Fearful women pulled at their petticoats in a form of intellectual agoraphobia. Caged birds once released do not always survive. Many late Victorian women believed that the cage that had securely protected them for so long was preferable to the exposure and vulnerability that stepping into the outside world could bring.

Whether in or out of the cage, women knew that they had a duty to support their husbands' position in society. In order to dress in a way reflecting the status of their male owners, women wore uniquely complicated clothes, excessively fussy and detailed. Furthermore, they found an increasing number of ways and opportunities to redecorate their persons. The true horror of the boredom of Victorian middle-class life can be seen in the way that a woman's day was proscribed and punctuated by the need to change her clothes. It would not do to be seen at 3.00 pm in the outfit suitable for 10.00 am.

Suitability demanded a change not only of clothes but of attitude for evening. Whereas days were tight-buttoned, nights were surprisingly nude – a Victorian woman at a ball was described as having neck and shoulders standing out like a champagne bottle from an ice-bucket. Obviously all this changing was as much a device to pass the time as a way of demonstrating the wealth and leisure that underpinned such conspicuous consumption – but it was more. Victorian domestic life was dedicated to detail. Fashion change revolved around an almost endless, continuous need to introduce new details – as if the female body were an animated Forth Bridge where no sooner had one detail been changed than up popped another ready for alteration. It was bred in the bone – and that is why domestic daily life was so utterly and precisely over-detailed.

Along with the love of detail went the even greater love of rules that governed detail. There were rules for every aspect of Victorian life and they were codified and clarified in an endless stream of books dedicated to etiquette. Not even the Versailles of Louis XIV had as many social dos and don'ts as the Victorians. Behavioural rules beget fear and the more there are the greater the fear, because the greater the chance of an unwitting *faux pas*. The paradox of etiquette manuals is that, whilst ostensibly setting out to remove that fear, they serve to increase it by revealing the complexity and irrationality of the game. For game it is – a particularly cruel and divisive one. In an upwardly mobile society such as that of the Victorians, where someone like William Hesketh Lever, born the son of a Bolton grocer, could become 1st Viscount Leverhulme well before his active life had finished, social insecurity was endemic. By making social rules as arcane and complicated as possible, the upper classes wreaked a sort of revenge on the *nouveaux riches* who were breathing down their necks. No zeal equals that of the convert, and once the *nouveaux riches* had managed to engineer their own place near the upper classes, they enjoyed the game even more, viciously twisting the knife of correct social usage in the ribs of the coming wave of upstarts. They, in turn, took their revenge and did the same to those below. The etiquette game thus became the game that all the classes could play, to greater or lesser degree. That being said, it was played with the greatest vigour by the middle classes – those who had the most to gain or lose from it. Middle-class society became a vast snakes and ladders board – a game invented in fluid and mobile social times: invited to dine with Lady Glencora, up the ladder; spill your wine, down the snake you go. The pleasures and the pitfalls were infinite.

'The Lady of Quality', one of the century's best-beloved tautologies, was at hand to guide the uninitiated and insecure through the jungle. Titles proliferated, from *Hints at Etiquette and Usage* to *How to Behave*, but all followed the same premise – that good society followed rules that had to be known, understood and accepted by those who wished to join the club. There were rules for every aspect of domestic and social life. To break them was to court social disaster. Some were sensible, and eased social intercourse. Most were foolish and constituted nothing more than childish traps for the unwary. Their main purpose was to give the middle-class woman, surrounded by servants yet chafing at her idleness and lack of purpose, something with which to pass the time. That was one thing – but, in such a restricted and codified society, it was essential to do so correctly. No area of life was too arcane to escape rules – in a *Little Book of Diversions* women were taught that 'the modes of fainting should all be as different as possible and may be made very diverting'. It was all to do with what, in another favourite phrase, the Victorians called the 'decencies of life' – and the need to keep a distinction between 'the little great', the patrician and landed aristocrat, and 'the great little', the mass of respectable aspirant members of the mercantile and professional classes.

It is easy enough to laugh at the manuals of etiquette, looking back from an age when society has reduced the social niceties to a minimum, but they were as essential a part of Victorian fashionable life as garments were – and in their nuances they changed almost as rapidly as fashion itself. Aimed at women who were insecure in their social role, they made their every footstep tentative and nervous, but their lasting effect was benevolent. Deprived of the public-school education of her brother, and denied the socially and politically educative influences available to her husband, the Victorian woman turned her back on the great issues of the day and cultivated her own sensibilities. The etiquette book was her first manual, but soon it gave way to her magazine or periodical, created exclusively for her and, as the century moved on, seen increasingly as her textbook for life.

Cynthia L. White, in *Women's Magazines 1693–1968* claims *The Ladies' Mercury* of 1693 as the first women's periodical. *The Ladies' Diary*, first published in 1704 and appearing annually until 1841, hoped to reflect 'what all women want to be – innocent, modest, instructive and agreeable'. The editor was a man, as most editors of women's magazines were in the eighteenth century, so in effect *The Ladies' Diary* was telling women how *men* felt they should be, but the prominence of social and moral instruction in the pages was influential right at the outset.

In eighteenth-century aristocratic circles women were considered the mental and social equals of men, even though their rights were tightly constrained. Their magazines reflected this. They were 'frank, vigorous and mentally stimulating . . . reflecting a broad spectrum of interests and activities'. Eighteenth-century women's magazines were patrician in tone and presupposed an intelligent, informed readership interested in an intellectual forum for discussion of any topics, not merely those ostensibly of interest to women. Such high ideals were dropped in the nineteenth century because, initially at least, middle-class women did not have the educational and social advantages of the aristocratic women of the previous century. In the early decades of the nineteenth century, 'women's magazines were no longer required to contribute to the intellectual improvement and advancement of women, merely to provide innocent and amusing reading matter . . . Women's topics became the norm, including increasing emphasis on fashion, homes and problems.'

The Victorian former public-school men who published and frequently edited such magazines, having outstripped their women in education, assumed that they had also done so intellectually. The assumption was as impertinent as it was erroneous, but it stuck. For decades, women's magazines have confined themselves to what men see as trivia, even though they, much more than women, need the attitudes admired by magazine editors. As late as the 1920s, a whining letter in *Woman's Own* summed up the childish self-centredness so frequently part of the male psyche when a male reader wrote, '. . . . I want a wife to listen to my troubles, to be ready and willing to soothe and comfort me . . . a wife whose first and only interest is me . . .'

Undoubtedly, women's magazines did much to trivialise women as well as perpetuating stereotyped roles for them. They encouraged Victorian women to create their own domestic empires to overcome the frustration of being excluded from the real one and, by doing so, developed an inward-looking pettiness in many of their readers. In that sense, nineteenth-century magazines can be seen as the mouthpiece of the Victorian male scam that women were better and more desirable because they were pushed to the parameters of a life which at its male-dominated centre could be brutal, hard and no place for a lady. As a magazine editor put it, with the degree of sentimentality required of the times, 'The heart is her domain . . . to watch over the few dear objects of real regard with an eye that never sleeps, and a care that cannot change . . .'

Of course, it was a disgraceful con, but out of it came good. The value of women's magazines in the nineteenth century can increasingly be seen in the forum they provided for educating the sensibilities and developing the morals of their readers. Men scoff at women's magazines as trivial, bourgeois and irrelevant but they can be seen as one of the great civilising influences on society. It can be argued that man's emotional growth was stunted in the nineteenth century not only because of public-school education but also because he did not have the equivalent of a woman's magazine to undermine its more pernicious influences and assuage his emotional needs.

It is fashionable now to scorn the problem page, but if women's magazines are manuals of behaviour (which they all are, even today) then the problem page is in every sense the magazine's heart. Would men still continue to follow the brutal and outdated stereotype of their sex if their insecurities and uncertainties about their sexual and social roles had been given the help that was received by women through the benevolent pages of their weekly magazine? Letters from readers (a stand-by of Victorian magazines, whether genuine or created by editors) and the answers they received inculcated attitudes that were essentially Christian. Similarly, the increased amount of fiction in women's magazines concentrated on stories with a strong moral charge. They offered guidelines in practical Christianity. As modern parables, women's fiction in nineteenth century magazines restated in contemporary dress the virtues extolled in the Bible.

As Victoria's reign reached its apogee in the late 1860s, the indoctrination – by men, by the Church, by magazines and novels – had succeeded. Every middle-class woman saw herself if not by birth, at least by demeanour, as the Perfect Lady. It is not easy for us today, when the term 'lady' is frequently used in a derogatory sense, to realise just how important it was for men and women that the female of the middle classes should be a lady – and be clearly seen to be so. Dress codes which, like etiquette books, are much more interested in 'Thou shalt not' than 'Thou shalt', laid down absolutely rigid rules about how a lady dressed. Cleanliness was a moral duty to Queen, country, lord and master. Vulgarity of dress was the worst solecism. Refinement and gentility were all. In practical terms, moral rectitude meant constriction and inconvenience in clothes. Gloves and shoes were worn as tight as possible; waists were nipped in, bottoms were padded out, and skirts were perversely inconvenient – huge, bustled or with long trains that a lady must never allow to drag on the pavement. To do so was to risk the assumption that she was a wanton. It was accepted that such visual extravagance would be equally extravagant in financial terms. *Punch* felt that by 1857, the high point of the crinoline, things had reached such a pass that 'ladies have to choose between a fine dress and a family, for no income but Rothschild's can provide for both.'

Such moral criticism was the typical male's reaction to a situation his sex had actually created. Women's dress was merely one part of the opulence and exaggeration of a period when man subconsciously vied for supremacy with nature, empire and the world. Naturally his wife must be dressed extravagantly, not only in order to keep her happy in her backwater and to assuage masculine guilt at putting her there in the first place, but to feed the essential emotion of the Victorian male – his pride.

For the public-school boy turned repressed man, the expense of a fashionable wife was a small price to pay for a surrogate outlet for his own frustrated decorative urge. Man gave up fashion in fear and left it to women with contempt. What he failed to see was the disastrous effects of his Great Betrayal – on himself, as well as on women.

THREE

Power Images

In 1988 a book was published about two women and the clothes they wore. It was concerned solely with their appearance. It suggested, without actually stating, that the women were rivals who dressed in order to vie with each other in fashionable extravagance. Remarkably, the book consisted almost entirely of pictures of the two women, presented in full colour and with little commentary, showing them enjoying themselves at Ascot and during The Season, touring, sightseeing and attending privileged occasions such as first nights and premières. The two women were invariably dressed to kill, in the most glamorous, Hollywood fashion. Despite their appearance, they were neither film stars nor models. *Royal Style Wars* was a piece of visual hagiography. Its subjects were the Princess of Wales and the Duchess of York. It sold 65,000 copies.

Royal Style Wars appeared to tell us more about their dress designers than about the Princess and Duchess but, by leaving so much out and yet selling so well, it actually told us most about ourselves and what we need from royalty.

Photographs of the royal family are endlessly in demand: formal – the Queen in evening dress, Garter sash and Orders; informal – the Queen Mother enjoying a day at the races; intimate – the Princess of Wales with her children at a school fête; caring – the Princess Royal with handicapped children in Africa; even saucy – the Duchess of York behaving rumbustiously on the ski slopes. Whatever the need, the royal family is happy to provide the image. They know that adulation cannot exist in a vacuum. We need images to enable us to create our concept of royalty. Without royal pictures the majority of us would have no perception of royalty either as an institution or a collection of individuals.

Before the age of the camera and the invention of photogravure, enabling photographs to be reproduced in newspapers, the appearance of royalty was known through images carefully chosen to flatter the concept and the king, available only through selected outlets. Royal private life could be kept private and royalty could have been (but rarely were) casual about their behaviour. People with an entrée to court circles paid for the privilege by being discreet about the private lives of kings. If Elizabeth I had slipped during a galliard there might have been titters and whispers behind her back after the event, but the majority of her subjects – those outside the tiny charmed circle of privileged aristocrats – would be unlikely to know anything about it. In those days, only good was spoken of kings – at least publicly.

For modern royalty, it is harder. 'Moles' and cameramen are everywhere. When the Duchess of York slips and falls on the pavement, not only do Queen Elizabeth II's subjects all know within hours; so does anyone else in the world who cares to be interested. To the chagrin of the modern royals, interest in their private lives is so intense that not even private events can be guaranteed safe from the prying lens. Photographers will crawl for hours through prickly undergrowth to train their zoom lenses on the Princess of Wales sunning herself in a bikini on what she thought was a remote and inaccessible beach. They do it because they know that royalty sells – and that we are the buyers.

Our greed for visual confirmation that the royal family is the way we could be if we had their money and advantages, coupled with our pathetic longing for them to be better than we are – more beautiful, kinder and more gracious – makes us eager to consume all images, whether snatched in a theft of privacy or permitted as an act of publicity.

The camera has presented royalty with a paradox. It has made them wildly popular by saturating us with images which are, on the whole, flattering, but it has also removed the right of veto they have traditionally wielded over such images. In the past, the royal image originated with a painting. The sitter exercised total control over his personification of royalty. If the portrait was not to his liking, it never saw the light of day. The camera needs no sitter. It does not wait for the carefully composed face to be 'ready'. It is cheeky, amoral and fast – like a pickpocket. The intrusive lens can do its work so speedily that the victim is not even aware that the act has been perpetrated.

While Queen Elizabeth I could – and firmly *did* – control the image of herself as Gloriana, it was the *process* of image-making that limited the numbers of people who could actually see that image. The original oil portrait was hung in only the grandest house; copies found their way into the lives of the lesser aristocracy; copies of those copies were made for the gentry. The scale of this dissemination was minute – as were the numbers who saw any version at all of the royal image on anything other than coins and, at a much later date, in highly stylised form as pub and inn signs. Prints made from the original portrait, authorised by the monarch, were popular, but the classes within which even they circulated were limited. On the whole, the upper and middle classes were the consumers of the royal image. Possessing a picture of the royal head was not simply a manifestation of their loyalty. They needed a visual talisman upon which to base their belief in country and monarch. They required concrete proof of the glory of kingship, in a way analogous to the visual evidence of the glory of God that they were given by religion. Popes and archbishops knew all about man as Doubting Thomas; they realised that belief in something as essentially insubstantial as they were peddling could not happen in the abstract. Images were vital for understanding. Churches provided them. Stained glass, statues and carvings gave ample proof of the reality of Christianity. Although not as amorphous as the concept of godhead, the idea of kingship was not necessarily easily grasped by a people subject to and restricted by a remote being in London.

It was recognised as essential that those at the apex of the triangle composed of people, aristocracy and crown should be familiar with the royal appearance whilst being kept in constant awe of it. Men are superstitious. It is hard to plot a ruler's downfall when his eyes stare hard at you from his portrait on your walls. His actual physical presence is an even greater deterrent. This belief provided one of the rationales behind royal visits to the houses of the great and powerful families of Elizabethan England. Even so, it was realised that a monarch must be more permanently exposed to the people who mattered – the people who could endanger his power. A king could not be so much a myth that mention of his name brought no physical picture to mind.

Visual reminders for the upper and middle classes were a part of the process of government and control. The lower classes, trapped and remote in their far-flung rural fastnesses, had no idea of how the monarch looked. Their loyalty was to the monarch's local surrogate – the squire or member of the rural aristocracy or gentry who virtually owned them, body and soul, on the monarch's behalf. When little children in their first week at a big new school are asked the name of their headmaster, they almost invariably name their housemaster. He is as far up the chain of command as they dare look. So it was for the vast majority of the Elizabethan population – the rural poor. They believed in the Queen, although unseen, because the squire, who *had* seen her, said they must, and his servants, who had seen her portrait, told them about her appearance as proof that she really must exist.

Portraits are commissioned; copies of them are made only with permission. Such limited visual sources allowed the court tight control over what was essentially a publicity image until well into the eighteenth century, when it collapsed. Royal dignity was assailed by the caricaturists who unleashed the dogs of ridicule to tear apart the carefully presented myth. Gillray's and Rowlandson's cartoons seem vicious to us now, but they were particularly popular with the middle classes, who were monarchists almost to a man. The royal mystique collapsed before the caricaturist's brush throughout the Georgian period and into the Regency. Apart from their physical inadequacies, the bovine attitudes, ludicrous liaisons and gargantuan appetites of royalty were exposed in the most unflattering terms, to the delight of all except the poor victim. Beau Brummell's gibe about the Prince Regent – 'Who's your fat friend?' – is almost certainly apocryphal. Even a man so limited that he would spend a morning in striving for the perfectly tied cravat (as we are told Brummell frequently did) would have sufficient about him to realise the consequences of such a remark, and yet Cruikshank's portrait of George IV shows how appropriate it would have been – appropriate and irrelevant, because the cartoonists were there first. Everyone knew how grotesquely the monarch's stomach had swollen.

The caricaturists exposed monarchy in a way undreamed of by their predecessors. The reason why they did so and were able to get away with it was that by this time executive power had departed from kings. Ridiculing them neither endangered the state nor unbalanced the body politic. Fox, Pitt, Shaftesbury – there were other, non-royal, men of power fighting to impose their will on a democratic country. Kings were already only for show. With the baleful reign of Queen Victoria which, in retrospect at least, seems to have been one long withdrawal from the realities of life, kingship finally became an ever more private obsession of the monarch – a puppet show with only limited public performances, mainly taking place on a very privileged secret stage from which the curtains were only occasionally drawn back.

Victoria's bizarre view of her role, her attitudes to her subjects and her paranoid insistence on privacy effectively took monarchy, in a century of increasing communications, back to the days of Elizabeth I as far as most commoners were concerned. Remote and distant, if not exactly awe-inspiring, she was rarely seen although, unlike Elizabeth I, images of her proliferated. Her head appeared on playing cards, the newly created postage stamps and even, according to the diary of a French traveller who visited Portobello market, on a condom – an unlikely privilege shared with Gladstone. At least everyone knew what she looked like. In this century, the royal family has until recently continued to view itself in the Victorian way, living a life removed from the people and, in return for vast material advantages (£25.7 millions per year of taxpayer's money for the upkeep of the Royal palaces alone), allowing itself to be seen and viewed formally when it wished to be, strutting and posturing as kings in a play.

Until the stand made by the tabloid press in the early eighties, virtually all royal images, on film or in print, were nothing more than formal records of formal sightings. Like strange rare birds, the royals flew into view, allowed themselves to be watched and snapped from a distance – and then took wing again. What happened back at the Palace was a secret as closely guarded as an osprey's nest – until the 'Wedding of the Century' (at which the heir to the throne married Lady Diana Spencer) made every month the open season for royal watching and enabled the popular press to take advantage of royal gullibility and lack of public experience. Deference is what keeps the royal charade afloat – the people's towards them and theirs towards the people who can ultimately remove them. After the 1981 wedding, both sides forgot.

It would be easy to blame the heroine of *Royal Style Wars*, the Princess of Wales, for single-handedly undermining the position of monarchy, but it would be unfair. The Duke of Edinburgh had done sterling groundwork with the inherent vulgarity and inappropriateness of his 'get your finger out' philosophy, as had his daughter Anne, now the Princess Royal, with her lack of sportsmanship that manifested itself in her telling reporters and photographers to 'naff off' when things were not going as she wished. Such language delighted journalists and public alike. No one at the Palace seemed to be aware of the old 'do as you would be done by' adage, and they seemed genuinely surprised when, by making Princess Anne even more unpopular than her aunt Princess Margaret had been, the press told her to do the same – and by doing so, said it to the whole of her family. The private puppet show was over. Every performance was public from now on, and nobody could keep the rabble out. Just as in any theatre, the costumes were an important part of the 'magic' and good performers were clapped and cheered, whilst bad ones received jeers and cat calls – for their clothes as well as their act. The royal sideshow had been launched and, although no one seemed at first to realise that this was to become a theatre of war, the more perceptive observers could detect whiffs of the theatre of cruelty as well as the theatre of the absurd.

Even today, only a minute percentage of the Queen's subjects ever see her in the flesh. In that, we are as Elizabeth I's subjects were. For most of us the reality of Elizabeth II is every bit as remote. She only exists in photographs and on film. Where we are at an advantage (or is it disadvantage?) is in the plethora of royal images that has flooded our consciousness through television and newspapers. Since the Wales's wedding the royal family has been chronically over-exposed and it is now a visual bore to all but the most rabid admirers on one hand, and sneerers and snipers on the other.

The paradox of royalty is that consistency breeds boredom and yet consistency is at the very heart of their existence. Because historically they have been judged only by their appearances, the image has had to remain as immutable as fashion and ageing will allow. In the past, it was essential for basic recognition; now, such consistency only cloys the appetite it feeds. We know the Queen's taste in clothes; we know her favourite colours but we do not know what she thinks or how loudly she laughs – or if, indeed, she laughs at all. She is all image and no substance, just as Elizabeth I was.

For Queen Elizabeth I the problem of over-exposure did not exist. The image was controlled, the sightings outside the Court extremely rare. The entertaining of ambassadors and foreign dignitaries were state occasions for which she dressed accordingly, sumptuous in velvets, jewels and gold, proclaiming the divine right of kings with every inch of her body. For Elizabeth II these occasions are middle-class business affairs devoid of glamour, politically irrelevant and constituting nothing more significant than possibly futile gestures of governmental good will towards other governments. To attend them, the Queen wears a plain woollen frock and carries an Asprey handbag.

For Elizabeth I, queenly appearances were Public Relations exercises of the grandest kind. Throughout her adult life, she presented a façade of monarchy that, despite her ageing, was not allowed to wither. In fact, both appearance and portraits were largely *trompe l'œil*, or even legerdemain, requiring the willing suspension of disbelief from all who saw her. She refused to grow old – or at least to be seen to grow old. One of the unnerving things about her portraits is the uncanny similarity imparted to them by her stylised form of dress. Those painted in the 1590s differ little from those of twenty years earlier. It was not a question of mutton dressing as lamb. She had never been a lamb in the first place. She was always a swan, dressed as the centrepiece of the banquet.

It was royalty, not vanity, that demanded such consistency of appearance. Elizabeth had created so strong a personal image that she could not allow it to change. The image of British royalty demanded the sustained illusion of an eternally youthful and powerful Virgin Queen, to be admired by ambassadors and complimented by courtiers as personifying the nation itself. And like the Queen's looks, the flattery had nothing to do with flirtation and everything to do with politics.

Although sixteenth-century Europe was racked by wars, it was moving towards a more settled political order and states and countries increasingly vied for diplomatic supremacy. Liaisons between royal houses were made for political and territorial gain. A virgin queen ruling a peaceful and prosperous country was an attractive matrimonial possibility, as Elizabeth and her courtiers well knew. The fact that suitors came and went, through the good offices of ambassadors, who might well return home bearing descriptions of the Queen that were at variance with the official image, did not matter – so long as they kept coming. By doing so they proved that England continued to be an attractive marriage prospect – and its queen worthy of flattery, despite her fading charms. Any prospective nuptials were purely political marriages between countries, not individuals, and Elizabeth presented herself accordingly. She advertised her country's prosperity by the grandeur of the receptions she gave for ambassadors, but above all by the magnificence of her presence. Lupold von Wedel, travelling through England in 1585, described the Queen as 'like a goddess such as painters are wont to depict'. On 27 December he saw her at Greenwich, 'being in mourning for the Duc d'Alençon and the Prince of Orange . . . dressed in black velvet sumptuously embroidered with silver and pearls. Over her robe she had a silver shawl, that was full of meshes and diaphanous like a piece of gossamer tissue.' A sighting of such superb plumage was pretty much par for the course.

André Hurault, Sieur de Maisse, who was ambassador extraordinary from Henri IV to Elizabeth, takes up the theme: 'She was strangely attired in a dress of silver cloth, white and crimson, or silver "gauze", as they call it. The dress had slashed sleeves lined with red taffeta . . . '; 'She was clad in a dress of black taffeta, bound with gold lace . . . and lined with crimson taffeta . . . She had bracelets of pearls on her hands, six or seven rows of them. On her head she wore a coronet of pearls, of which five or six were marvellously fair . . . '; 'She was clad in a white robe of cloth of silver, cut very low . . . '; 'This day she was habited . . . in silver tissue . . . She wore innumerable jewels on her person . . . about her arms and on her hands, with a very great quantity of pearls, round her neck and on her bracelets . . . ' This was Dynasty dressing in the modern as well as the traditional sense of the word.

It was not just foreigners and ambassadors who were to be impressed by all the magnificence. Elizabeth wished her own people to see her bejewelled and richly lacquered person as being as inviolable as the state. Thomas Platter describes her at Nonsuch in 1599 as 'most lavishly attired in a gown of pure white satin, gold embroidered, with a whole bird of paradise for panache, set forward on her head studded with costly jewels, wore a string of pearls around her neck and . . . was most gorgeously apparelled.' She was sixty-six at this time and could hardly have been dressing for sexual allure. Instead her attire proclaimed power – her country's and her own. Those who saw her were impressed with both. De Maisse describes her at the age of sixty-four: '. . . save for her face, which looks old, and her teeth, it is not possible to see a woman of so fine and vigorous disposition . . . ' Paul Hentzner described her a year later as '. . . very majestic; her Face oblong, fair, but wrinkled; her Eyes small, yet black and pleasant; her Nose a little hooked; and her Teeth black (a defect the English seem subject to, from their too great use of sugar); she had in her Ears two pearls, with very rich drops; she wore false Hair, and that red . . . '

For those who could not see her in person, there were the portraits. Magnificent, even awe-inspiring, icons to the glory of her secular power, they impress as intended, through the extraordinary care lavished on the detail of her dress, which frequently draws the eye away from the plain and rather severe royal face. Not that the representation of her beauty was expected to suffer. A proclamation drafted by Sir William Cecil in 1563 makes clear the Queen's determination not to let things run out of control. Painters, printers and engravers must take the royal likeness from 'some speciall conning paynter' who 'might be permitted access to hir Majestie to take ye natural representation of hir Majestie whereof she hath been allweise of her own riall disposition very unwilling'. It continues, 'hir Majestie will be content that all other paynters or gravors . . . shall and maye at ther pleasures follow the sayd patron or first portraictur.'

Portraits of the Queen, with their insistence on the magnificence of her dress, reflected the showy vulgarity of the times. The Renaissance arrived late in England – well over a hundred years after it had become a force on the Continent – but its effects were electrifying. It brought a new vitality and strength to the arts, and linked England with France and Italy both spiritually and intellectually. The court of Elizabeth's father, Henry VIII – confident, prosperous and peaceful – had been rich. Reflecting the monarch's personal vanity, it had been fashionable – lavishly, even excessively so, with grotesquely impractical codpieces and unexpectedly practical detachable sleeves, which featured heavily in Henry's wardrobe. Following the King's lead, the art of male power dressing had reached a high point of display, with men puffed out like pouter pigeons, their clothes slashed, slit and patched in a manner that had come to England from Germany, which, surprisingly enough, was a fashionable conduit at the time. Slashing quickly became a crude visual symbol for masculine lawlessness and brutality before being tamed by fashion into visual shorthand for male power. Its origins were with the soldiery, as many fashion innovations are.

The collapse of the feudal system towards the end of the fifteenth century, and the fading of the chivalrous ideal, left European rulers dangerously exposed. They had no people to fight for them. Nobles were no longer able to raise armies by levies of their own peasants. Standing armies did not exist. Rulers were forced to rely for their armed forces on ruffianly bands of mercenaries who knew no loyalty, gave no quarter and were available to the highest bidder. Lawless itinerants, they wandered Europe and were arguably more dangerous unemployed than when actually involved in fighting. Known as *Landsknechte*, they were first raised by the Holy Roman Emperor Maximilian I. Roistering in their power and strength, barely controllable even by the harshest discipline, they were the Hell's Angels of their time. Unlikely as they seem as style innovators, it was the *Landsknechte* who gave the sixteenth century its most singular male fashion.

Swiss mercenaries, having plundered the costly tents of their conquered foes, used the material to patch their battle-torn clothing. Inexpertly sewn, or even merely pushed through the gaping holes, the patches fluttered and moved in a way entirely appropriate for these free-living characters whose crude masculinity seemed a grotesque parody of male strength. Of course, their appearance was noted, as was the illusion of strength and freedom that it gave them. A fashion was born. When it was taken up by German soldiers, the fashion was made. Desperate attempts followed to stop a style that seemed to be cocking a snook at all decent folk and the modesty of their dress. Slashing was seen as dangerously sexual and provocative – mainly because it was associated with the mercenaries who were feared (and yet perhaps admired) for the impunity with which they raped and plundered their way from country to country. There was something salacious about clothing with slits. It alarmed the authorities, as sexuality usually does. In 1518 the Austrian Provincial Diets tried to stop ripped-up clothing, and in 1525 the University of Tübingen forbad slashed hose. Their attempts were useless, and the fashion leaped like wildfire across the courts of Europe, finally arriving at Henry VIII's in London, where its vulgar macho connotations endeared it to the flashy monarch.

If Elizabeth I was to be the personification of queenly magnificence, she had learned the lessons of dress from Henry VIII. His appearance represents power dressing at its most raw and powerful. He was, to transpose a comment by Carlyle, 'clothed not only in wool but with Dignity and a Mystic Dominion'. Not that Henry stopped at wool. One would hardly expect that of the man who, at his meeting with Francis I in 1520 at the Field of the Cloth of Gold, between Guines and Ardres, changed his dress twice a day and wore nothing but 'silver damask or tissue of silver, cloth of gold and other costly materials', as Max von Boehn records.

Henry's wardrobe was sumptuous not simply to flatter his vanity. He subscribed to the view held by his royal peers that kingship was not only magnificent – it had to be paraded as magnificent. Further, he believed in sumptuary distinctions, reserving certain materials and colours for exclusively royal use. A year after he had succeeded he decreed that silk, gold and purple were to be reserved for royal wear. Realising that, for its own safety, some of the privileges of even absolute royalty must be granted to a certain degree to its closest and most loyal supporters, he ruled that, in addition to the royal family, tissue of gold was allowed outside the charmed circle, but only to dukes; sables to earls and above; satin and silk to barons and above. Crimson and blue velvet were to be reserved for members of the Order of the Garter.

Henry enjoyed the trappings of monarchy. His reign was enlivened by every kind of splendour and display. He delighted in masques, tournaments and jousts. He was handsome – the ambassador Sebastiano Giustiniani reported: 'His Majesty is the handsomest potentate I ever set eyes on . . .' And he was rich. He understood and gloried in his power. He dressed to impress, following the latest Italian and French fashion, as well as the slashing of the Swiss, but he knew he was a parvenu compared with other European monarchs. The Tudor dynasty had existed for less than fifty years. He was, in terms of heritage and breeding, *nouveau riche*. That is why Henry VIII was vulgar. Even on quite ordinary occasions he could not help flaunting his power and money. Ruby-encrusted chains swung from his neck, diamond brooches sparkled in his bonnet, and his fingers glittered with rings heavy with previous stones. He was the original medallion man, a prince of Bel Air transposed in time to the Tudor court.

Von Boehn describes the inventories of Henry's wardrobe. It included 'coats of blue and red velvet lined with cloth of gold; the doublet of purple velvet, with sleeves to match, thickly embroidered in Venetian gold, presented to him in 1535 by Thomas Cromwell; and much else besides'. He goes on to say that 'at his first meeting with the Princess Anne of Cleeves the King wore a velvet coat so richly embroidered

STRIKING ATTITUDES

Men and women with power – temporal, political, social and sexual – dress to proclaim their position. Even those with spiritual power cannot resist dressing the part, as portraits of bishops, popes and cardinals make clear. The army has been especially susceptible to dressing up. Napoleon and his generals had many a happy hour designing uniforms with the right amount of military 'swank' and the dress of the Prussian army in the last century was the talk of officers' messes across Europe. The officers of the Amsterdam Crossbow Civic Guard known as 'The Meagre Company' primped and preened for Frans Hals' brush as wholeheartedly as a model girl flirts with the photographer's lens. These men are in love with their lace, gold trimming and taffeta sashes every bit as much as a model girl in an evening dress by one of the great couturiers.

70

DIGNITY AND IMPUDENCE

When Top People take time off, they like to do so in surroundings that inhibit lesser folk from attempting to join in. As this picture taken at Lord's cricket ground in 1906 shows, the tempo of breeding at the turn of the century was slow and clothes were designed to keep it that way. Long skirts dragging across the grass, large flowered headwear and tall top hats removed the wearers from the hurly burly of everyday life.

However the City Gent is occasionally prepared to make a public spectacle of himself in front of the plebians, if it is for a good cause. Of course, he is a member of a privileged tribe just as many of the people at Lord's, but he wears the suit of authority, and that is his carapace against the jibes of the world.

POWER PACKED

When world recession bit deep as the nineties dawned, designers became desperate over falling sales. They turned in many directions for new inspiration. Suddenly, clothes previously only seen in specialist clubs, magazines and brothels were paraded down the catwalks of the fashion centres of the world – and were greeted with enthusiasm.

MASTERFUL MALES

Power, so the myth goes, is the ultimate aphrodisiac – but it must be appropriately clothed. The top hat not only protected the lordly head, it projected his superiority over the commonality of mankind by adding as many as six impressive inches to his height. The significance of the riding crock could hardly be lost on the dimmest tenant farmer. He knew that, when his lordship dressed to kill, it was not just the fox over which he intended to have the whip hand.

The modern working class man of might does not have such an arsenal at his disposal. We are all inclined to assume that the clean-cut, well-dressed man is going to be less brutish than the man in the dirty sweat-stained vest. It is a false assumption.

RIGHT ROYAL ROBES

The appearance of Prince Charles is in sorry contrast to that of his illustrious ancestor, Henry VIII. Whereas Henry appears every inch the King, Charles looks no more distinguished than a banker. The dilemma of modern royal dressing is a real one: how can a prince look the part without seeming like a character out of a fancy dress parade? As it is, the heir to the British throne is totally devoid of the glamour traditionally associated with princes and kings because he does not have the right everyday dress with which to clothe his majesty. The fact that such dress is reserved for atavistic ceremonial occasions pinpoints the irrelevance of royalty in the modern world.

in gold that the ground of the material was no longer visible; it bore buttons of diamonds, rubies and pearls'.

Behind the arrogance of frequent wife-changing and his refusal to accept the ruling of Rome lurked a man deeply unsure of himself, politically, socially and even, perhaps, sexually. This would explain his compulsive need for display. The weakness behind the show-off and bully is known to us all. But, whatever his motives, Henry VIII dressed in order to parade unequivocally the power of kingship. His success in so doing was total. His figure in Holbein's paintings has become an archetype not just of royal magnificence but of overt masculinity. Even when his youthful beauty faded and his figure spread, Henry's broad shoulders, muscular arms and strong legs describe the outline of the male as powerful warrior. What we can never know is how much such an image was a figment of his own imagination, forced upon his artists, who were made to exaggerate his looks and his dress in order to produce the icon that such a junior dynasty felt it required, but what we do know is that his arrogantly straddling figure has become an archetype of the temporal pride of kings.

Although by no means an archetype of masculine power in Henry's mode, Louis XIV was very much the personification of royal power and, indeed, of the fashion leader. He was the most absolute monarch that Europe has ever seen. Versailles life was neurotic and inward looking. Everything hung on the smile or the frown of the King. Courtiers cringed, fawned and waited to be told what to do, what to think and, above all, what to wear. Once the King declared a fashion, it was compulsory. No exceptions were made – not even for the Queen. He ruled his courtiers rather as a bad nanny dominates the nursery: by privileges granted and removed at whim, always overshadowed by the threat that they can disappear through an unwitting transgression caused by rules changed without warning.

Such a world, be it nursery or court, usually revolves around favouritism, and Versailles was no exception. Louis XIV not only corrupted his court by encouraging his favourites (what absolute monarch has not?), he displayed them with all the blatancy of James I and his coterie of chosen young men at the English court. He created a privileged group of fifty 'special' courtiers who were allowed to show how special they were by wearing a coat unique to their number, with the right to wear ornamentation – silver, lace and embroidery – banned for other courtiers. This was more than a uniform – it was a badge of servility – but it had the highest in court slavering for the privilege of wearing it.

Although towards the end of his reign Louis, influenced by his homely mistress Madame de Maintenon, later his morganatic wife, began to favour plainer clothing, Versailles, at the height of his excess was the most fashionable court in the history of monarchy. It amazed the world. Crowned heads came eagerly to see it, having ensured that they were dressed with sufficient grandeur to at least hold their own, even if they could not hope to compete. Queen Christina of Sweden arrived in 1646 accompanied by a retinue dressed entirely in yellow and black, with costly silver lace, in an effort not to be upstaged.

The magnificence of kingship still had to be recorded, and so it was throughout Europe. Hyacinthe Rigaud and Pierre Mignard were kept endlessly busy with portraits reflecting the grandeur of Versailles. Van Dyck painted Charles I forty times and Queen Henrietta Maria thirty; Velasquez constantly painted Philip IV of Spain, and Rubens produced a stream of portraits of the Infanta Isobella. These portraits, like those of Henry VIII and Elizabeth, emphasised the importance of kings and the opulence of courts but, above all, they highlighted the theatricality and drama of monarchy – and suggested the dangers. Dressing up and playing a part – seen most obviously at the Trianon in Versailles – was becoming more important than the realities of rule in most of the courts of Europe. Kings and princes displayed themselves on an elaborate stage for a privileged and besotted audience; they heaped excess on to audacity by performing as themselves in masques – plays within the play of daily life – and ballets; they pushed the common generality of folk further and further from the enchanted circle. The laughter of that circle drowned the rumble of the tumbrel's wheels. Having been given every opportunity to make kingship work as government, it was the monarchs themselves who destroyed the ideal by committing *auto da fé* in their exquisite costumes. The eighteenth century effectively saw the death of the state led and ruled by royalty. It was killed by the running sore of privilege which had become a suppurating wound from which drained the life blood of kings and princes who preferred enjoyment to responsibility. By their inability to recognise and cope with the new forces sweeping across Europe, they condemned kingship, where it survived, into becoming little more than a puppet show to amuse the crowds, whilst the work of government was carried on elsewhere. It was the beginning of the retreat of hereditary privilege which has continued, somewhat jerkily, up to our own time.

The effect on fashion was enormous. In the days of Henry VIII and Elizabeth I fashionable dress had taken its place in the hierarchy of power. Both monarchs dressed in the height of fashion. The richness and extravagance of their apparel made manifest the magic of monarchy. Rich stuffs, vibrant colours, embroidery and jewels not only proclaimed the power of wealth, they also betokened the grandeur of rule. They exemplified the difference between the court and the rest of the country. Courtiers dressed to vie with each other and to gain the royal attention. By dressing magnificently (often beggaring their estates to do so) they perpetuated the myth of a king made man-god, surrounded by acolytes who in their appearance seemed barely of human clay.

Just as kings, courtiers were rarely exposed to the view of the peasants. But those who saw them – household servants, grooms and gardeners – would have described in wonder the swaggeringly ostentatious dress of someone like Edward Sackville, 4th Earl of Dorset, bejewelled and beaded, wrapped in gold and pearls, whose person, according to Clarendon, was 'beautiful, graceful and vigorous'. Indeed it was, showing the privileged appearance of a man with a decent bed on which to rest his head, and a table groaning with good food. His upright carriage would contrast cruelly with that of his peasants, bent double with arthritis, faces scoured by sun and icy wind, and bodies ravaged by malnutrition. Ground down in poverty and endless work, they must have looked on him as a being from another planet. What the peasants did not know was that the appearance of so many courtiers was little more than a carapace – albeit glittering and magnificent – to hide the inadequacies of the man inside. The 3rd Earl of Dorset was notorious as 'a licentious spendthrift', and Clarendon says of Philip Herbert, 4th Earl of Pembroke, that he had no other qualification than 'to understand dogs and horses' – and yet their dress actually convinced that they were capable of the grander roles that birth and corruption made possible for them.

The insensitivity of ostentatious Elizabethan dress – proclaiming so clearly the difference between the few who had everything and the many with nothing – showed the contempt of the aristocrat for anyone not in his fortunate position. Fashionable dress was, then as now, a weapon of class war. Behind the magnificence of court dress lurked a mood both menacing and sinister. Underneath those sumptuous black velvets and glowing pearls, death waited. These clothes proclaimed a power that was, quite literally, of life and death over the beholder – even when the beholder was of the same class.

Murder, plotted or resulting from violent disagreements between ruthless men, was no out-of-the-way thing in Tudor court circles. The aristocrats who dressed so magnificently were like bizarre insects or reptiles who use their covering and colourings to instil fear as well as to attract. Their superb appearance had little to do with self-indulgence or sexuality. It was about self-proclamation. It said, with an incontrovertible voice, that here was a class ruthless in its power and its determination not to lose that power – a class appropriately clad in clothes for killers, the dress of death.

The Elizabethans have left us the strongest images of apparel as politics. Their clothes said 'Keep off' to anyone who might have designs on a courtier's position and privilege. They were as essential a proof of status as his prodigious house and armies of richly caparisoned retainers. Extreme as their dress frequently was when an extra effort was required to outshine other contenders for the monarch's favourable smile or the influential ambassador's hand clasp, it was never ridiculous. Power, nakedly paraded, is never laughable. It always instils fear and that is precisely what the fantastically decorative clothing in portraits of the time was meant to do. Those within the court looked at each other's finery with nervous, speculative and awe-struck eyes; those outside the court – the middling and little people – gazed in terror at what such magnificence meant in terms of ruthlessness and disregard.

The collapse of kingship killed it all. It was a death hastened by another force that began in the seventeenth century, became a power in the eighteenth, and swept all before it in the nineteenth. The middle-class merchants, businessmen, and lawyers who were excluded from the charmed circle of the court nevertheless wished to emulate its customs, manners and fashions. Their attempts to keep up with courtly privileges narrowed the gap between monarchic magnificence and the garb of the rest. Elizabeth I, rigid in heavily embroidered velvet and stiff with pearls, was so extraordinarily out of the ordinary in her appearance that no one would dare question her right to be queen, but, by the end of the seventeenth century, the dress of kings differed very little from that of the fashionable upper classes.

Once fashion had ceased to point the uniqueness of the monarch and the extent of his power, it lost much of its strength. No longer meant to strike awe and wonder into the beholder, it became the province of the self-obsessed, the narcissistic and vain, who believed that fashionable clothes exclusively brought superiority over others. The fashionable man was born, and the power of clothes was diminished. Monarchs had once worn their extravagant clothes not to make them *feel* superior, but to proclaim their *actual* superiority. Now a king who cared about his appearance had become just another fashionable figure, a mere member of the snobbish classes.

As he slid down the scale of magnificence, his people, the insultingly named commoners, came up until the two met in the sartorial desert of pretty clothes with no other purpose than to make the wearer agreeable to look at and acceptable to the social classes that based their judgements on appearances. By then the merchants had become the magnates and the lawyers the judges. Their power could no longer be taken away at whim. They eschewed fashionable dress. The man of power no longer needed clothes that proclaimed his power. Fashionable dress – and an interest in it – increasingly came to be seen as silly, shallow and self-indulgent. By the end of the eighteenth century, extreme fashion had become something to be laughed at. By the end of the nineteenth, all fashion had been put in that most laughable of all categories – a woman's interest. Cast out by intelligent and educated people, it has stayed in intellectual limbo ever since. Emotionally, however, its pull is as strong as ever.

Whereas in the age of kings power dressing meant being in the forefront of fashion, as magnificently showy as money could afford, government by bureaucracy was carried out by men who had deliberately turned their backs on fancy clothes and the latest styles. For every Disraeli, who shared with Boy George a penchant for wearing extravagantly jewelled rings over his gloved fingers, there were hundreds who believed their role as politicians far too serious to be undermined by the levity of fashion. They increasingly distanced themselves from the extravagance and self-indulgence of court circles, preferring to submerge personal preference in uniformity. By the nineteenth century a wave of woollen darkness had submerged and obliterated what was once described as 'the jolly glitter of sequins'. Democratic power was dressed in sober rectitude. But there were exceptions. In the eighteenth century Carl Philip Moritz was shocked that members of the House of Commons came in wearing 'their great coats and boots and spurs', adding that 'some crack nuts, others eat oranges' during the proceedings – a telling example of aristocratic privilege showing its disdain for fashion and propriety.

Glamour was left to society – the court grown large. It dominated London throughout the eighteenth and nineteenth centuries. As the court had done, society revolved around appearances, but now all they proclaimed was social position and wealth. Powerless, the members of such a society were as vulnerable as butterflies. Known only for their fashionable appearance, they could be obliterated by one lapse of taste. As Prince Hermann von Pückler-Muskau said, 'Brummell once ruled an entire generation through the cut of his coat.'

When the king's new clothes ceased to set him apart from his people, and he was no longer perceived as undoubted ruler, he became just another part – and not always even the head – of that fashionable society. In their fall from grace, kings dressed increasingly like their subjects. With rare exceptions – Edward VII and Queen Alexandra, Edward VIII – few members of royal houses have initiated fashions and many – Victoria, Queen Mary and The Queen Mother – have dressed quite outside current fashion movements. Whether fashionable or not, as ever greater numbers of their subjects could afford to dress in costly and extreme styles, royalty was left with only the quality of its jewellery to show its superiority.

Even that distinction is now removed. Queen Elizabeth II and the House of Windsor have a collection of jewellery without rival. It is all real. Nevertheless, it can be upstaged in design and impact by fake costume jewellery. The royal collection is priceless but, on a royal occasion when other women are wearing jewellery worth a fraction, it fails to tower head and shoulders over the rest. The jewels neatly encapsulate the modern royal dilemma.

Apart from consciously atavistic occasions, such as the Garter Ceremony, which are straightforward costume drama, there is no way that the royal family can divorce its appearance from that of its subjects. Any attempt at self-conscious historicism causes laughter – as both of this century's investitures of the Princes of Wales have shown. The exciting, original and awe-inspiring effects that Queen Elizabeth I could create with her appearance are lost for ever; no male member of the royal family can recapture the dangerous glamour of Henry VIII.

Of course, the major reason is that dress has changed so much at all levels. Sobriety and comfort – never serious considerations in power dressing in the past – are the bedrock of all modern dressing, including that of royalty. The gap between the style and magnificence of dress of the upper and middle classes has narrowed; the distinction between town and country clothing has blurred; the working classes are no longer malodorous and drab; the need for power to proclaim itself by sartorial ostentation has gone.

We are all kings now – the gap between them and us, formerly so clearly demarcated by clothing, has closed. Furthermore, we have changed the nature of fashion. The majority of the Queen's subjects could dress as she does, achieving the same effect at a fraction of the cost. Young women could dress as the Duchess of York and the Princess of Wales – the *Dynasty* look is freely available in high-street chain stores. But whereas royalty is trapped in an historical formality, increasing numbers of ordinary people see modernity and fashion in terms of relaxed, casual dress. Bagehot, in his analysis of the lore of royalty, published in 1867, suggested that mystic reverence and religious allegiance are essential to a true monarchy. When kings ruled, such emotions were created and sustained by a consciously regal appearance. When a king is indistinguishable from his subjects, the willing suspension of disbelief is put under enormous strain. As Eric Gill pointed out in *Clothes*, published in 1931, 'The counting-house sets the fashion now. All men wear the clothes of the puritan man of business . . . ' The mystique has gone, leaving royalty no alternative but to be pretty little puppets, cleanly and neatly dressed in out of date clothes.

When kings ceased to rule, the power equation was altered. Clothes ceased to be part of the formula and were left in the limbo that *Royal Style Wars* so clearly delineates. Fashionable dress became part of the inconsequential world of snobbery that was all that royalty could hold on to when its power fled. It is a world to which they are confined even now, marooned, like fashion itself, on a plateau of vacuity where appearance without power makes puppets of them all.

Class Wars; Class Work

Class is about relationships. How we relate to our fellows and their values both depends on and affects how we view their class and the ways in which it differs from our own. We see them as a reflection of how we see ourselves and our own social status. A consciousness of class relates us directly with primitive man. Class distinctions – real or imagined differences between social groups – are the basis of a modern tribalism which, like primitive tribalism, is a compound of hatred and fear on one side and pride and strength on the other.

Tribal distinctions have always been shown by niceties in dress and body ornament. In North America, Indian tribes decorated their bodies in unique ways so that Hopi would not be confused with Sioux, and neither of them could be mistaken for Chinook. Quakers, Amish folk and Hassidic Jews proclaim the religious attitudes that separate them from the rest primarily by their appearance.

Dress is *the* social shorthand, unequivocally proclaiming what we are, where we belong and, even more important, what we are not. It reveals at a glance our attitudes, values, ideologies and standards. Above all, it proclaims our tribe. The impulse to keep the tribe pure, to exclude those who do not share the tribal blood, and to banish those whose behaviour dishonours that blood, means that primitive societies do not readily allow the introduction of members of other tribes into their enclosed world.

Class distinction works in the same way. Exclusivity by class, however, is not so clear-cut as exclusivity by blood and its distinctions cannot be so effective. A tribe is an extended family, with loyalties to individuals and entity that brings a homogeneity much stronger than that found in tribes formed by class. Primitive tribes are based on contentment and pride. Members accept the tribal hierarchy and have no desire to move up, or out, of the pattern. Advancement within the tribe is not sought, but bestowed.

Modern class tribes lack the dignity of their primitive counterparts because they contain within themselves the elements of discontent and non-exclusivity. Although ordered at their centres, there is always disruptive activity bubbling away at the edges, where movement beyond the ill-defined boundaries separating one class from another might take place. In the traditional upper, middle and lower classes – the rulers, the bourgeoisie and the workers – there is always the possibility of movement up or down, though the former usually involves a struggle and the latter only occurs after a fight or a failure. At the peripheries of classes, the cement that binds the centres crumbles under the pressures of fear and loathing.

Chauvinism is the basis of tribalism. Class attitudes are chauvinist in the most literal way. To fear and loathing can be added envy and discontent. Members of one class see more advantages in the next class and wish to enter it. Their efforts are traditionally met with attempts to foil them. Only the determined succeed, and the first sign of their impending success is when they start dressing in the clothing of the class to which they aspire. The person who lives in a bedsit in Kilburn and dresses at Ralph Lauren is saying, 'Forget the unfortunate financial solecism of Kilburn, I'm a Chelsea-Golf GTi-M4-weekend countryman at heart, and will be in *reality* when I get enough money.'

Behind the simplistic and broadly-based conclusions that the eighteenth century was dominated by the upper class, that the driving force in the nineteenth century came from the middle class, and that the present century has seen the rise of the working class to political and economic power, there lies basic truth. Of course, we know that the middle class were exerting considerable power in the eighteenth century (and even before) and we accept E.P. Thompson's contention in *The Making of the English Working Class* that 'the working-class presence was, in 1832, the most significant factor in British political life'; but as a broad rule-of-thumb the traditional pairing off of centuries and classes works.

It does so for reasons that are social rather than political. A class moves into ascendancy, it would seem, in two stages. It becomes a political force and then, over a period of anything up to a hundred years, develops into a cultural one. The dominant class at any moment is the one that has the greatest hold over behaviour and attitudes in all aspects of life. A class becomes an entity when it can be seen to hold different attitudes from those of other sections of society, and it becomes the *dominant* entity in that society when it imposes its attitudes on the rest. As the twentieth century ends, it is possible to observe the emergence of a group large and powerful enough to be sufficiently dominant to warrant being considered as a fourth class. This class is not merely new; it is an entirely different sort of class. It threatens in the next century to sweep aside existing classes and to take complete control of society.

The 'class' is youth, and its present position is analogous to that of the rich in the days when most were poor. Just as those who had money were powerful and those who had none were not, so, in the future, those who have youth will hold the power and the rest, the aged, will be powerless. The twenty-first century will see the old tripartite class distinctions swept away by the force of the youth class which already largely ignores traditional class barriers. In their place, we will have a dualist society: the young and the old, as distant and mutually hostile as rich and poor in medieval England.

At the moment the equation is incomplete, as not everyone who is young is rich or everyone who is old is poor. But if youth and age are to take the place of the traditional rich and poor division of society, eventually the young will all become wealthy, having made the old impotent by ensuring that all desirable aspects of life are only available to the young, who are beautiful, healthy and filled with physical power. Ageism will be developed to provide the philosophical rationale for the process. Already 'old' is entrenched in the language as a pejorative adjective. Although horizontal, the youth class will initially include the three vertical classes, as it does now, but eventually the old snobbery of traditional class distinctions will disappear under the new snobbery of age distinction.

A society can be foreseen which will work from a new base. For the first time since ordered societies emerged, the have/have not distinctions based on wealth will be irrelevant. There will be no possibility of betterment by scrambling over one class to another. Everyone will start in the youth class and everyone must leave it. Once a system based on age, not wealth, is established then everyone must eventually become *déclassé* – at the age at which society considers it necessary. The traditional patterns of class movement will no longer apply.

Already there is enough evidence that young people have sufficient shared characteristics to be considered an entity in the way traditional classes have been. As a broad group, they measure up as a class: they are bound by shared ideologies; they hold as virtues attitudes considered vices by other classes; they betray hatred and fear for those who do not share their attitudes and, above all, they have in abundance the bedrock of class distinction – self-interest. They exhibit all the characteristics of the old aristocracy.

At the moment those members of the youth class who are wealthy hold different views from those who are not. They subscribe to traditional ruling-class views whereas the attitudes of the 'have-nots' are more akin to those of the anarchic working classes of the nineteenth century. But already there are sufficiently strong shared cultural attitudes – towards music, drugs, sexuality, human rights and wars – to see a homogeneous youth class emerging inevitably in the future.

Class distinction relies on shared educational attitudes, moral values and ideologies as much as on social and economic aspirations. Clothes, in James Laver's phrase, represent the furniture of the mind, and the youth class, like the historical classes, will display its common aspirations most clearly in the way it dresses. It will signal its superiority over the age class without needing to flaunt financial status. Rejecting the automatic status of wealth that dominates class distinction at the moment, youth class status will be based on things money cannot buy – health, beauty, vitality and individuality – which will be communicated through dress. The embryonic signs that a youthful appearance is the desired appearance – Jane Fonda, Rosemary Conley, work-outs, gymnasiums, health clubs – are already with us. Their influence and its effect on appearances will be discussed later. First we must look at how such fundamental changes have come about.

Class distinction proclaimed through dress is as old as dress itself. It is impossible to have one without the other, unless everyone is forced to wear a uniform and barred from altering or adding to it in any way. Such distinction is less obvious today than in the past, but it still exists. As the grosser inequalities of civilised life are removed for greater numbers of people, distinctions through appearances become less obvious, but differences in philosophies of life perhaps become clearer.

Thorstein Veblen, in *The Theory of the Leisure Class*, points out that 'the greater part of the expenditure incurred by all classes for apparel is incurred for the sake of respectable appearance.' What has traditionally been striven for is an appearance that will be considered respectable within not only the individual's class, but also among the class he admires. Sumptuary laws, whereby monarchs and rulers attempted to control and regulate what each class and manner of man could wear, failed – as they were bound to do. No sooner was an item of clothing, type of cloth, trim or colour proscribed for certain people than they wanted it more than ever. As legislation, these attempts were as futile as they were persistent. They were regularly imposed from the fourteenth to the seventeenth century and they always failed. They did not take into account human nature and its desires. Like Prohibition in America during the twenties, sumptuary laws could not win, because the human need for what was banned was too great.

Sumptuary laws have gone, but the desire to control and manipulate what people wear remains, and where laws fail usage succeeds. We do not need statute books to apprise us of what is correct dress within our circle. Subtle, unwritten – even unspoken – rules do the trick. No upper-class man needs to be told that grey leather shoes are a lower middle-class form of dressing, any more than a lower-class man needs to check that a white riding mac is inappropriate for his class. The silent sumptuary laws of class may not be codified but they are ubiquitous and they work on our attitudes to dress in every particular. And they always have. Fashion is a code, a symbolic language, as Tom Wolfe has pointed out. And each class adds something to that code when it has its period of power.

The influence of the upper classes in the eighteenth century and the effects of the

THE PANOPLY OF POWER

Ever since man first perfected his trapping skills, fur has been prized. It was coveted not only for its warmth and tactile qualities but because it betokened power and wealth. Kings made it an integral part of their royal dress for formal occasions, having their robes lined and trimmed with ermine and sable. But, commoners could not resisit copying, from Russian merchants to American railroad millionaires. Women adored fur. It not only gave them status, it outlasted everything else in their wardrobe.

IN CHARGE
(previous page)

The man who steps aside from the pressures of society and appears
to write his own story is seen not as a coward running away from a world that is too tough for him but as a hero who has kicked the system. That is why cowboys as portrayed in romanticised form on the screen have become such enduring folk heroes.
James Dean in 'Giant' created a powerful image of a man in charge of his life, and even young people born long after his death identify with his style.
Jeans, denim and cowboy boots are the clothing of those who yearn to throw off society's constraints.

SOCIAL SOLECISMS

Enclosed societies always evolve their own rules of suitable behaviour and there are often rules that those outside that society find hard to understand or accept. For well over a hundred years, debutantes were insiders in society just as homosexuals have been outsiders. The season was their reward for accepting the prospect of a lifetime of being second best and acknowledging that upper class life was run for, by and around the needs of the male. When, in 1957, the Queen withdrew from the Season, part of the ritual was still observed. At Queen Charlotte's Ball, the debutantes continued to curtsy, not to the Queen but to a vast birthday cake.

The gay world is also conscious of inequality, but in their case it has little to do with wealth and much to do with their basic rights as citizens. Many homosexuals believe that they should be able to marry just as heterosexual couples do. To raise consciousness of this issue a mock marriage was staged in London in 1991 for the benefit of the cameras. The debs bare their shoulders in a gesture of subjugation, they wear gloves to signify that they do not toil, and coronets to indicate their wealth and status. As for the gay wedding, are we meant to infer that two men cannot marry and live together without one of them wearing drag and the other assuming fancy dress?

CROWNED IN GLORY

(overleaf)

Etonians wear hats decorated with flowers to celebrate the fourth of June. Their resemblance to crowns seems entirely appropriate for young men who expect to inherit the earth and be rulers of all they survey.

THE BACKWARD GLANCE

The gentleman's suit has remained essentially unchanged for about a hundred years. Robert Redford in the 1974 film, *The Great Gatsby,* plays a character living in the 1920s. The suit designed for him by Ralph Lauren is exclusive to neither date, and could be worn today without causing comment. It is a reflection on moribund men's dress that the suit looks current seventy years after its time whilst the Rolls Royce is old fashioned.

middle classes on nineteenth-century dress suggest that discomfort, impracticality and inconvenience in clothing bestow distinction. The distinction, of course, is that between the workers and the idle. In times when servants are plentiful, they do the sweating, heaving and hauling for those who can afford to employ them. In centuries when labour is cheap, as in the nineteenth century, the servant class swells enormously. It has been estimated that the million female domestics recorded in 1851 were largely employed by the middle classes and the dress of the middle-class female of the time bears out the supposition. The women who, relieved of domestic chores, flocked to the Crystal Palace for the Great Exhibition did so in clothes that conspicuously proclaimed the fact that they were not required to work. The point was not only made by their rich silks and satin brocades: the ruching, flouncing, ribbons and flowers that rioted over their figures drove it home in that they clearly needed the full-time ministrations of a lady's maid. Even more obvious an indicator of idleness was the hooped skirt, revived after almost a century and precursor of that most conspicuous proof of leisure, the crinoline, soon to come in all its ostentatious glory. Its form curtailed movement and made strenuous exercise impossible. It literally incapacitated women for work.

Fashion commentators look to the past in order to find illumination for the present. It is largely a pointless exercise. Earlier centuries can give as few clues to the present as the study of animal behaviour can reveal the secrets of *Homo sapiens*. In both cases, the gap is too great. The changes that have taken place in society between 1892 and 1992 are so enormous that we look in vain for comparisons. Standards of behaviour, morals and education have changed radically. The legal and social position of women has altered dramatically. The roles of master and servant have been blurred. We are almost looking at two different species. Above all, the position of the young has changed out of all recognition. No longer condemned to be little adults, they have become people in their own right – and with their own power. The age of waiting in order to be taken seriously has dropped considerably in the last hundred years – and is still dropping today.

Before the young had become a power, the working class had, early in the twentieth century, exerted its influence on society *and* attitudes to dress. Edwardian fashion – long trains and tight waists for women, and stiff collars and constricting armholes for men – marked the final glory of the conspicuously leisured classes. Even before the First World War it had become apparent that the social drone and butterfly were endangered species. The supply of domestic workers that had seemed so prodigal, making possible endless physical idleness, was drying up, diverted from service to other, less demeaning, ways of making a living.

The change in middle-class life styles was first seen in women's dress. Workers' clothing inhibits efficiency if it is tight and constraining. Workers had learnt centuries earlier that if they were not efficient, they were not employed. The lesson was soon learnt by women who increasingly had to take over the running of their homes. Fashion quickly reflected the new roles. Elegantly long skirts had been routed even before the First World War, but uniform killed them off for ever as daywear. By the twenties, the whole shape and silhouette of women had changed. While the number of women who fulfilled the Flapper stereotype was minute – the young and privileged – all women's clothes loosened up and became less constraining as a result of flapper fashion, following the mood that already existed for ease of movement. Even Queen Mary's silhouette became slightly more relaxed in response to the general trend. This fundamental change – looser and shorter – was the first step in fitting women's dress for modern, active lives.

Men's fashion took longer to loosen than women's for two reasons. The main one was simply that the change in the male workforce was not so cataclysmic as in the female.

97

The boss class and the office worker continued after the First World War much as they had before. Constrictive clothing was enjoyed as a perverse self-discipline – the discomfort of leadership – and a proof of status. It was, after all, little more than school uniform writ large for most middle-class men. Any child prepared to accept the idiocies of dress current, for example, at Eton in the twenties, could surely come to terms with the minor illogicalities of adult dress away from the factory floor. It was a badge of class distinction just as much as the Eton collar.

Whereas workers' blue collars were soft, white 'boss class' ones were stiff. Whereas workers showed their braces, clerks proudly sweated, convention not allowing them to remove their jackets in the office, regardless of the heat. Even as late as the thirties, stiff white cuffs – the sartorial equivalent of the quill pen – were common in commercial offices.

The second reason for so little change was that male working dress having been 'set' in the nineteenth century – and not being required to change to accommodate a new situation as had women's clothing – it was only in casual dress that the new working-class freedoms could manifest themselves. The soft collars, looser trousers and pullovers instead of jackets that crept in during the thirties were the result as much of the increasing influence of sports as the lesson learnt from the clothing of the manual worker. As the appearance of the man of substance softened, so he transferred the stiffness of prestige on to his personal servants and unwittingly made them the future arbiters of male fashion and upholders of outdated conventions in masculine dress.

There is hardly a man who has not been brought face to face with the crassness of his sex in the form of a servant in a hotel or restaurant who is ostensibly paid to assist the diner, but will do so only if the diner conforms to antediluvian ideas of what constitutes gentlemanly dress. A tie and a conventional jacket are insisted upon so that the diner might avoid offending his fellows. Such 'dress codes' could be easily laughed away with the rueful thought that restaurateurs grow fat, with our connivance, on such follies, if they did not signify a much deeper malaise in the male sex. The foolish flunkeys who bar the way to a man without a tie will also allow a woman to enter wearing whatever she likes. They make the sexist assumption that women do not count as they rarely pay the bill and they mistakenly imagine that a man without a tie will be working class and likely to turn into a yob after a few drinks. There is hardly a hotel dining room or cocktail bar where these assumptions are not still held. The cynical social attitude betrayed by such an approach – demeaning to women and working men alike – is a true reflection of the views of millions of middle-class men. They are prepared to accept censorship by servants because of insecurity and a fear of being assumed working class. They forget that the suit and tie are also the hallmark of the criminal classes. The Kray twins were never seen in any other clothing, nor are the City embezzlers and property speculators who, despite their immaculate appearance and perfectly modulated tones, inhabit the sinister world of the super-crook.

Fear is one of the strongest motives for comformist dressing. By their attitude to dress, men have shown themselves the fearful sex. They will wear a tie and jacket on the hottest day in order to enter a restaurant with a woman who, by contrast, appears semi-nude, because they are afraid of being taken for non-gentlemen. Perversely, the discomfort makes them feel superior not just to women but to all the lower members of their own sex whose good sense in dressing to fit the weather debars them. By behaving foolishly they proclaim that they are gentlemen, and perfectly happy to be ruled by servants rather than savants.

Such gentlemen are, at long last, a dying breed, but until very recently they were the only breed that counted. One reason why the ease of the working man's dress took so long to have any effect on fashion was the determined refusal of the ruling class to stop seeing him as either a laughable yokel or a sly rogue, and to allow him any romance. Working-class sexuality has been the horror and despair of the other classes for centuries, and the working man, with his drink and debauchery, a danger to all decent women. A male hero from the workers did not emerge until the novels of Hardy, and a sexual one had to wait for D.H. Lawrence, but the true breakthrough was not literary at all. It came from Hollywood. Films of the twenties and thirties showed an egalitarianism conspicuously lacking in literature. As befitted the first truly popularist art form, film broke down the prejudice against the sexuality of the proletariat. It showed that working-class young men were not all mindless thugs any more than their girls were wantons. It created working-class heroes such as Spencer Tracy and Clark Gable who could never be taken for gentlemen and yet had enormous sexual charisma for middle-class women. Historians of fashion talk much of the influence of the Prince of Wales on how men chose to dress before the Second World War, but his effect was minute compared with the influence of the Hollywood heroes and their clothes. They spearheaded the move towards relaxed, non-status male dressing that James Dean and Marlon Brando carried on, to be universally copied by young men – and copied again from them by a new generation of actors like Harrison Ford and Matt Dillon.

Wars are great confidence boosters. People who survive previously unthinkable stress and overcome their fears frequently emerge from the ordeal much more assured than before. In the fifties the postwar effects on the young working classes began to be seen. Girls no longer dreamt of being able to afford to dress like their posh friends' mums; boys did not want to look like the boss at work. The youthful move towards egalitarianism had begun. We are so used to 'prides' now – Gay, Women's, Black – that we forget that the precursor, and probably the most important, was Working Class Pride. It came from the young working-class heroes of countless films and novels, from the working-class crooners and musicians but, above all, it was given the impetus that created the youth movement by a fundamental shift in the educational system.

Comprehensive schools are now seen as the great postwar educational failure, but as far as social and class advancement are concerned they should – and probably could – have been the success of the century. In the past twelve years we have witnessed a government ruthlessly determined to discredit and destroy the comprehensive system. The credibility of comprehensive schools is probably gone for ever. But comprehensive education has played a crucial role in the formation of the emerging youth class by building on Working Class Pride and, for the first time, advocating that there are no educational betters to be aped. Grammar schools, by copying the standards and approaches (not to mention the syllabus and uniform) of the public school, sub-scribed to the view that nineteenth-century public-school tenets were suitable for mass education in the twentieth century and therefore to be emulated – a view that, despite clearly reflecting the most insidious class prejudice, was untrue in the most practical and pragmatic terms.

For the young products of the comprehensives there were no distant role models from privileged backgrounds. They were their own role models. They no longer felt socially inferior. Almost as if to confirm it, the whole world suddenly wanted the culture that their education and class had spawned; popular music bewitched all classes, even though they were never allowed to forget with which class it originated. Comprehensive education, for all its manifold faults, helped change the class structure by giving confidence to the traditional underdog class and, by doing so, helped lead the way to the fourth class. Even though the educational experiment has ended in ashes, its effect on social history has been permanent and beneficial.

The new confidence in being working class *and* young manifested itself most conspicuously in music and dress, since the mid-sixties the leitmotivs of youth culture. Youth must bait authority – and authority must rise to the bait – and both have done so thoroughly in the last twenty-five years. Youth has scrawled the writing on the wall in order to frighten, in Tom Paine's phrase, 'ye who sit at ease and solace yourself in plenty . . .' Like latter-day Luddites, the young have used their culture to show their intent to smash the class hegemonies of the past. If the last two centuries have witnessed the slow retreat of privilege, the end of this century sees the institution of the greatest, unearned, privilege of all: that of being young. Its effects on appearances have already been considerable.

Ever since fashionable clothes ceased to be about power and became merely the dressing of sexuality, the dignity of age has been threatened by the impertinence of the 'latest fashion'. The reasons are obvious. Elderly, or even middle-aged, sexuality has a degree of ribaldry about it, if not in practice then certainly as an idea when considered by a nonparticipant. Dressing in a sexual fashion means drawing attention to the body – or, at least, areas of it – as something to inspire desire. Clothes are created in order to make the body desirable. Fashion assumes a body of perfect proportions and preservation. Anyone who has passed into the age of sexual anonymity – for most people, in their early fifties – when walking in public no longer excites a provocative or even speculative stare from the opposite sex, dressing in such clothes is likely to render them risible. Who hasn't smiled at the middle-aged man who has carefully folded his fat into tight blue-jeans? Or again, the elderly woman in the supermarket, with immaculate make-up – lipstick too red and eye shadow too deep – and carefully contrived hair, who excites pity or contempt but rarely the sexual desire her appearance might suggest she craves?

Fashion is, almost by definition, ageist. Shakespeare's Seven Ages of Man are still with us. The shuffling old man no longer wears pantaloons but the proof of his sexual collapse is in his bottle-shouldered cardigan. Young men proclaim their potency in cleverly engineered suits with built-up shoulders. The visual assumption is that the *real* man – still able to get it up – has square shoulders to remind us of the hidden power between his legs, ready to become as prominent as the shoulders at the slightest encouragement, whilst the droop of the old man's shoulders tells its own sorry tale.

The problem of age, sexual desire and clothing is worse for women because they are more vulnerable to fashion change. Many allow their make-up and hair to freeze in the style of what they see as their moment of optimum attractiveness. The results of such thinking can be disastrous. We are all familiar with the woman in her late fifties who still dresses and makes up as if in her early forties, with outdated styles and colours. Make-up and hairstyles are especially treacherous traps as they change most rapidly and are always altered in order to sell new lines to younger women.

Older people, it is assumed, cannot follow the extremes of fashion and preserve their dignity – but why should this be so? There is no preconceived 'suitability' inherent in any style. Only usage makes rules. There is no logical reason, for example, why men should not wear skirts and make-up, except that we as a society have agreed that men do not do so. In his polemical pamphlet, *Trousers and the Most Precious Ornament*, published in 1937, Eric Gill argues passionately that society's decision to force man into trousers is a threat to his virility: 'any protuberance by which his sex might be known is carefully and shamefully suppressed. It is an organ of drainage, not of sex. It is tucked away all sideways, dishonoured, neglected, ridiculed and ridiculous – no longer the virile member and man's most precious ornament, but the comic member, a thing for girls to giggle about . . .'

As it ages, the body becomes a reminder, in the words of H.G. Wells, that 'humanity is but animal, rough-hewn to a reasonable shape'; it is a shape that many men and women are unhappy to accept. Secret pacts with hairdressers, tailors and dressmakers have, for generations, been the stock in trade of the fashionable man or woman who is as afraid of growing old and dropping out of fashion as of losing sexual attractiveness. In *Heartbreak House* Shaw has one of his characters admit 'I was brought up to be respectable. I don't mind the women dyeing their hair . . . it's human nature. But it's not human nature to tell everybody about it.' Why the old should feel shame about disguising the effects of age is a mystery. Why they should feel shame at growing old is less so. Sexually, society has always resolutely echoed Longfellow's words – 'Youth is lovely, age is lonely' – to the extent that we all believe that it is, literally, a shame to be old. Such shame exists as part of the greater shame felt by vast numbers of people who have an interest in fashion and yet are terrified to admit it.

Fear of fashion is a paranoid intellectual state. It strikes even those whose jobs depend on it. Recently, the Woman's Page editor of the *Guardian*, whilst reporting on Paris fashion shows, actually wrote, 'please don't call me a fashion editor' – which for double-standard sauce is equivalent to someone writing about an art exhibition and prefacing his comments with the old 'I don't know anything about art but I know what I like' cliché. Another woman, writing in the *Evening Standard*, took exception to fashion pictures being featured on news pages in newspapers. She felt that to give fashion such importance was 'positively insulting' to women, though she failed to provide an adequate explanation of how and why.

Such views are as commonplace as the commentary they normally accompany. As informed reflection on fashion they can be ignored but, as pointers to the intellectual paradox of men and women dressing for maximum attractiveness in deference to the mode of the moment (as every feature journalist does) and then belittling that mode and its importance, they are of some interest. They lead us to the heart of the problem that so. many people find with their interest in fashion. It is a problem rooted in the puritanism of the English psyche. It reflects our inherent fear of vanity – but it does more. It shows that even in the last decade of the twentieth century, after generations of free, universal, compulsory education we have not laid the ghost of our bodies and their sexuality. The taboo against showing-off is as strong today as it was when we were illiterate and uneducated.

It was the body that lay at the root of the fear of working-class sexuality; the body that made Black Power seem so terrifying; it is the body that makes us so nervous of lesbians and homosexuals and, above all, the body that makes age seem so disgusting. It is also what makes intelligent people admit to the vanity of their clothing. For now that fashionable clothes and power have permanently parted, what else can adornment be but a glorification of the body and, therefore, the feared sexuality that haunts us all? Longfellow's couplet could be extended to read 'Youth is lovely, age is lonely, brain is worthy, but body not.' Except, of course, that it is. We are all obsessed with our bodies and how to beautify them with make-up, face lifts, work-outs and everything else in our power. That, however, is not the sickness in our psyche. It is rather our shame at responding as humankind always has that demands self-analysis.

It is no accident that men, the sex least at ease with high-fashion dress and overt care for appearance, should be least at home with their bodies. Preening and flexing in the locker room has to be disguised as a pantomime; 'man's most precious ornament' has to be metaphorically detached from the body and treated jokily as a close friend. It is personalised with a name – Willy, Charlie, Fred – and treated as a 'good ol' boy'. It is inconceivable that women would treat the vagina in such a way, calling it Edna, Betsy or whatever. It can be argued that the difference in attitudes is little more than a result of physical geography, in that personalising something external comes more naturally than personalising something internal, but I believe its source is simpler even than that.

Men need to divorce themselves from their penis and treat it as a friend for whose actions they cannot be held responsible because it can be embarrassingly unpredictable. But behind the jokes lies the feeling that the most precious ornament might be more important than the body to which it is attached – the man is only as good as his best friend. If it is strong, he is strong. Such simplicity of thought has often led men to dress to emphasise their assets – usually fraudulently. From codpieces through tightly-cut pantaloons to the pop star's notorious shuttlecock, man has tried to make himself appear more of a man than is perhaps the case. The history of male dress suggests that men might well be more at ease with their bodies if they could remove the unpredictability from their penises – if they were permanently erect or even foldaway contraptions that neatly tucked away inside the body when not in use.

Women also suffer – different – feelings of physical inadequacy and, like men, have taken more or less fraudulent steps to overcome – or at least disguise – them. Since the sixteenth century moralists, usually male, have railed against the artificiality of female appearance from false accretions to the universally condemned 'painting'. The vanity of false hair, padded bosoms and made-up faces was condemned as a sin against God by Philip Stubbes in 1585 in his *Anatomie of Abuses* where he railed against women and 'the horrour of their impieties and tragicall abuses layd open to the world' ending with a plea that they 'leaue of their wickedness, call for mercie at the handes of God, repent and amen'. Even today, there is a residual distaste for an appearance too artificial. Whether or not such artificiality is morally reprehensible does not matter here. What is of interest is that, despite the criticism, the practice and the perceived need for it carry on.

Why was it considered that women needed physical help and men did not? Was the decision made by men or women? Would the status of the sexes be different now if both, or neither, had used 'paint'? Does it all relate to the male fear of the decorative urge that made him turn from kingfisher to crow in the early nineteenth century and made him eschew make-up even earlier, or was it motivated more by woman's fear of ageing and thereby losing her protector and financial support? Whichever, overt artificiality is now considered a feminine characteristic, to be indulged by men but not indulged *in*. The mincing fop with his painted face is seen by both sexes as a threat, but the interesting thing is that he who paints feels that he must also mince. Even when defying convention, man is conventional. So convinced are we that use of make-up is an exclusively feminine characteristic that men who use it feel that they must take on the other characteristics of the sex in gesture, manner and walk. Boy George and his friend Marilyn parodied the movements and mannerisms of teenage girls with dramatic success, turning themselves into animated Barbie dolls – and, like real Barbie dolls, only girls found them attractive.

In the early eighties the cult of decorative extravagance hit the London club scene. Fancy dress became *de rigueur*. Club boys began to wear make-up in a camp, female impersonator way. As the decade progressed, however, the masculine boy became the new icon. Tough and hard, with firm pectorals and tight muscles, he stared challengingly from the pages of *The Face* and *iD*, the very antithesis of the pansy and the poofter. He was not effeminate. That his narcissistic love of the male body frequently found expression in homosexual activity was unimportant. Working-out and body building are essentially homo-centric occupations. Gymnasiums are centres of sublimated homosexual desire. It was inevitable that, having achieved the perfect body, such boys began to use make-up to overcome facial inadequacies. However, they used it not to make themselves feminine, but to make themselves more beautiful in a masculine way. They brought to the streets – admittedly rather specialist, urban streets – what pop stars had brought to the stage ten years earlier; the glamorous illusion of physical perfection.

Make-up for men is still far from common, still associated with homosexuality, and still continues to be met by society's disapproval, but it is more likely that it will become commonplace than that make-up for women will disappear. It is part of the increasing beautification of the male appearance, and as such is unstoppable. More important, it is a manifestation of the determination of the youth class to smash the rigid stereotypes that have for so long bedevilled the sexes. It is not that young men wish to be like women. It is that they refuse to accept the patronising of both sexes inherent in the idea that certain things are suitable for women and others for men. How quickly attitudes can be changed has already been demonstrated. Less than a generation ago, a man who wore an earring – if he was not a gypsy – was proclaiming his homosexuality; similarly, a man who bleached his hair. Now both are seen as perfectly unexceptional – and, significantly, totally heterosexual – forms of self-decoration. Could there be a future when the majority of men – like the majority of women – wear make-up and do not cause comment? I feel that the evidence of the past suggests that there could and will.

The Daily Telegraph of 18 February 1991, carried figures from an Apex Trust report suggesting the size of the hurdle still to be overcome in our attitudes to sex. A survey of public and private companies revealed that firms are more likely to employ a murderer than a sex offender; 58.3 per cent of private sector companies said they would not employ a sex offender 'under any circumstances' and 33.9 public sector employers said that such a crime was 'an absolute bar'. The report, *The Hidden Workforce*, pointed out that 'Sexual offences were considered the worst type of offence . . . followed by offences against property, violence, fraud/forgery and robbery.' Such reports highlight the fear of sexuality that affects every part of our lives, especially our attitudes to our bodies and how we clothe them.

No Sex, Please; We're British, the title of a successful play, sums up perfectly the sexual attitudes of the British. 'Separate Sex, please; We're British' would be even nearer the mark. We seem incapable of incorporating sex into our daily existence in any profound sense. We stand apart from it and refuse to accept that it can be a part of our lives. That is why we have so many taboos, especially in our clothing and appearance. Taboo breakers make us nervous. We cover our embarrassment with laughter. When Vivienne Westwood, no slouch in the game of ruffling bourgeois feathers, hits at our sexual insecurities, our response is not to examine the insecurity but to laugh at the person who exposed it. People consider Westwood a madwoman, and prefer to ignore what she is pointing at.

Laughter to cover embarrassment is not new. It is a way of distancing ourselves from a situation, of putting an idea in parenthesis and tucking it safely away. It is because we fear sexual clothing that we parenthesise it. Men are afraid of the feminine side of their natures. To control the fear, they dress up as women. The greater their fear, the more grotesquely they parody femininity. We are all familiar with the drunken rugby team pushing a pram for charity, wearing enormous false breasts, stridently coloured wigs and crude make-up coarsely applied. We are meant to laugh at this – and we do, women as well as men. For men, it is a cathartic experience by proxy, temporarily cleansing and ridding them of their femininity and, in many cases, their fear of women. When women laugh, they are debasing themselves and their sexuality before the superior power of the male sex. On the other hand, when women dress up as men we do not laugh. They ape men at their most streamlined, elegant and sophisticated. Wearing top hat, white tie and tails, the woman impersonating a man is paying homage to his physical and social superiority. She is trading up.

The history of theatrical cross-dressing shows this fundamental dichotomy. Pantomime dames parody older women. Their shorthand for laughs is grotesque: either skeletally thin, with knobbly knees and huge feet, or pneumatically rotund, with unruly breasts and vast backside. In both cases their clothes are a pastiche of an extreme fashion now out of date – minis when skirts worn on the street are long, or platform soles when real women are wearing flat shoes – and their make-up and wigs are even more bizarre than those of the charity rugby team. Contrast the principal boy – who is of course a girl in this topsy-turvy world of misrule. No matter what the period of the pantomime, her dress is always the height of eighteenth century upper-class fashion, with tricorne hat, lace jabot and elegantly fitted velvet coat with flared skirt. But there the pastiche ends. The legs are never concealed and always end in high stiletto heels. Eighteenth-century upper-class fashion is chosen as the most feminine, or least overtly masculine, male dress that can be plundered from history. The result is a strangely glamorous and attractive hermaphrodity that would unsettle in a realistic medium – as Annie Lennox's appearance did on TV a few years ago – but is considered 'normal' on the pantomime stage.

Female impersonators either follow the grotesquery of the pantomime dame, in a parody of male fear and hatred of female sexuality – huge breasts, thwacking thighs, immense beehive hairdoes and tackily shiny evening gowns – or actually attempt to look like real women, dressed in the height of evening glamour. In both cases – exemplified by Ruby Venezuala of Madam Jo Jo on the one hand, and Danny La Rue on the other – the invariable period of fashion chosen to guy is the glamorously feminine fifties. The period is not without significance. The fifties was the last decade when women were able to be kept in their place, as men saw it, and dressed accordingly. It was the last time women wore gloves and hats as a matter of course in their pursuit of physical attractiveness rather than, as now, in parenthesis whilst making an out of the ordinary statement of elegance for special occasions such as weddings. It was, in many ways, the last time that women really wanted to look glamorous in a pampered, luxurious way. It is the period in which most men would have preferred women to have stayed – looking beautiful but biddable; their femininity shackled by long full skirts, trammelled by tight waists and constrained by stiletto heels. Deliciously feminine women, perfectly safe and unlikely to rock the boat of male superiority, their passing is still mourned by many.

Youth put a stop to that happy masculine dreamworld. When, in the seventies, women first decided to get tough to get the message across to recalcitrant men, they borrowed, not like Judy Garland or Liza Minelli from the elegant masculine evening wear of the thirties, but from the rough-cut world of the working-class male. Leather jackets, jeans and Doc Marten's are not glamorous on men, and are even less so when worn by women. They were chosen deliberately to say 'fuck you' to all the male attitudes still denying women equality of esteem, and to all the men who really wanted no more involvement with women and their attitudes than they would if playing with a Barbie doll. Those punk girls who startled us all were dressed for war, but the battle went awry because their sisters were afraid of the narrowness of the future they offered.

Male attitudes have not changed enough. Women are still seen by far too many as second-class citizens who can be given pretty clothes in order to keep them happy, and then largely excluded from the male power world. The post-Feminist male has many battles to fight to keep his hegemony, but he will eventually lose them all because there has been a fundamental shift to equality where it matters: on the level of youth. It would be as ridiculous to assume that there are no male chauvinists under twenty-five as it would be to imagine that there are no non-chauvinists over thirty. What has changed is not men, but women. Having thrown away their bras and make-up in the seventies, following a path no doubt as necessary as it was narrowing, they have taken them back – with an enormous difference. They are now perfectly prepared to present themselves to the world in the fullness of their femininity – not as a badge of inferiority to men, not to bolster sagging confidence, but to proclaim independence and assurance in their youth and attractiveness. The effect this is having on the other sex is already beginning to show.

With young men increasingly proud to be considered pretty and young women happy to be physically strong – even muscled – there has been a change in the equation of attractiveness. That change has shifted the basis of fashion. Whereas in the past it could be said with some truth that clothes made the man, clothes are no longer enough. As the youth class marches into the twenty-first century, health and vigour are no longer merely the basis for a fashionable appearance; they actually *are* the fashion – and shibboleths are already being moved to accommodate the fact.

Until very recently the idea of fundamental physical change to our body for vanity rather than health was anathema to most people. Superficial, short-term change in response to fashion's apparently endless need for new bodily shapes was perfectly acceptable, provided the medium of change was clothing not flesh. The basic body was sacrosanct. Bustles, corsets, make-up and all the panoply of *trompe l'œil* that fashion could muster were permitted – although frequently lampooned by frightened men and quasi-intellectual women – but the cosmetic surgeon's knife was taboo. Recourse to it was normally kept a closely guarded secret because to go to such extremes in order to maintain the façade of youth would be condemned by society as shallow and vain. Now, by making people more eager than ever to remain young-looking and reap the rewards denied to those who look old, the youth class is overthrowing the taboo and creating a new form of fashion change – body fashion.

Fashions must have their courts and the court of the coming cosmetic body fashion is found in southern California where the virtues of youth, vitality, beauty and the perfect body have always been extolled. Film lore has long said that a star must be young and sexually desirable, at all costs. As a friend of mine, a professor in Los Angeles, used to joke, 'L.A. newspapers are the only ones in the world without obituaries. You're not allowed to grow old here, let alone die!' Body surgery is becoming almost as normal there as buying new clothes is in the rest of the world. Californian dreams of eternal youth and the new youth class have together turned the body itself into the new fashion battleground. Instead of changing the cut of your clothes, you will, in future, change the cut of your flesh.

Are firm pectorals 'in'? Have plastic ones implanted. Does next year's nose need to be tiny? Have a bone chop. Too fantastic? Laughable? Ignoring basic common sense? I think not. As the premium on youth grows in strength, as surgery becomes more skilled and the use of drugs for control of the body more specific, body fashion will become as flexible and changeable as make-up is today. By the end of the twenty-first century, it could well take the place of changing the style of clothes in keeping the diurnal round of fashion moving. It could even prove to be the knock-out blow for clothes as the primary form of fashion.

QUESTA MAGLIA COSTA
£268.000

FIVE

Dressed to Impress

Pride – Prejudice – Sense – Sensibility – Persuasion: Jane Austen's titles read like a check list of the motives for fashionable dress and the ways in which we assess people through their appearance. We know that pride and prejudice are engendered by finery. We accept that men and women who are expensively or fashionably dressed will be proud of their money and taste that mark them apart from the rest. We take it for granted that they will be prejudiced against those who are not so fortunate, as well as against those *more* fortunate who are able to be even more ostentatious in parading their wealth and refinement on their backs. We have enough sensibility to pretend to disapprove of the 'If you've got it, flaunt it' approach, even though it has been the basic attitude of fashionable life for as long as there has *been* a fashionable life.

The sense of superiority that comes from being part of a fashionable coterie – privileged in money and status – is as alive and well as it was in the eighteenth century, as a cursory glance at *Tatler* or *W* makes clear. Pride and prejudice are, if anything, stronger in this century of egalitarianism than they have ever been. Dressing for privilege is part of the general effort to persuade that such privilege is a birthright which, if not quite inalienable, is to be seen as hard to remove and even harder to share in. It is part of a confidence trick to which most people outside the charmed circle gladly subscribe. So abject is our subservience to privilege that such a sharp delineator of society's peccadilloes as Jane Austen could have used Privilege as a title for a novel.

The emotional stranglehold that the Royal Family has on all classes is ample proof not only of our great respect for privilege, but of our positive need for it. 'Glossy' magazines and 'quality' newspapers assume that the icons of social inequality and assumed superiority must be paraded to persuade us not just that the hierarchy is safely in place, but that it is actually there for the good of all. The Season, once the major marriage-market of the English upper classes, who worked for future aggrandisement even whilst enjoying present privileges, has diminished in importance but, like an appendix, hangs on in the ungrumbling social body that carries its weight. Initiated in the late eighteenth century, the Season was traditionally inaugurated by Queen Charlotte's Ball, where aristocratic girls assumed the status of débutantes by curtsying before the monarch. The gravitas of the occasion was severely diminished when Queen Elizabeth II stopped attending, thus forcing grown women to curtsy before a substitute. Revealingly, it was a large white cake, sweet and sugary, that was selected as a suitable and convincing replacement for a crowned and anointed head.

It wasn't just that they were all having so much fun that made it impossible for even the upper classes, the most loyal of subjects, to follow the Queen's decision and give up the nonsense. The deb industry meant money as well as fun. But it was even more. The

Season which the debs graced had become the most blatant statement that the class system was alive and well and firmly held in place. It had an air of historicism (spurious, in fact) and, despite Queen Charlotte's Ball, it had the added protection of continued royal involvement and, therefore, tacit approval from most classes. It was part of a carefully managed tradition that had, like the monarchy, become so well entrenched that it was unquestionable. Ascot and Henley were (and are) seen as being as archetypally British as roast beef. To criticise them would not merely be churlish; it would almost be treason. Although the concept of royalty has become as questionable as the beef industry, its critics are still treated as if they have Mad Cow Disease.

In any society, those who hold power continue to do so only if they have cunning. The ruling classes in Britain (not necessarily synonymous with those elected by a gullible populace in order to be governed) decided in the last century that they must find ways of putting up a smokescreen to hide privilege and exploitation. People in power know the political importance of dress. If something as offensive to thinking people as outright and unearned privilege is being paraded, it must be clothed in disguise. This is why the upper classes, as wielders of social power, are so obsessed with the niceties of 'proper' dress as betokening correct form. It is one of the most arcane areas of social censorship because only those on the inside know the form. Dress is an adjunct to rule. It keeps people in their place – even those who feel secure. *The Times* in 1913 criticised members of the Order of the Bath who, despite their social distinction, had 'shown a deplorable inability to dress themselves properly.'

It was, therefore, to dress, the most powerful weapon in the class war, that the British turned when evolving privileges into a form where they became institutions as immune from question as the morality of the Archbishop of Canterbury. They opted for fancy dress in order to disarm criticism, knowing that the nation would accept virtually anything as long as it was properly clothed and disguised. There are, after all, over 6,000 registered Morris dancers in this country, a figure that must be as worrying as it is incomprehensible to anyone who believes that spurious dressing-up traditions carried on as a diversion from the political realities of late twentieth-century life can do nothing but menace our future in the twenty-first. But the British love fancy dress and they are happiest when their world is turned into a costume drama.

Blazers and boaters for Henley are an invention of Victorian times – a period when many English traditions were being invented to hide the fact that the most-trumpeted tradition, fair play, was being forgotten in the everyday lives of ordinary people. Top hat and tails for Ascot are no older. They have frozen as fashion has moved on not because they are the most practical or suitable form of dress, but because they are so closely associated with the events – and, more important, the class for whom the events were originally created – that they immediately betoken a level of privilege and confidence that precludes others. It is only in recent years that hiring such 'togs' has become a possibility for all men, of any class.

It is an interesting social pointer that the desire to ape one's perceived social betters is not removed, or even weakened, by greater education. Increasing numbers of lower middle- and working-class men choose to wear the trappings of a past and defunct upper class, if not for Ascot, then for the more everyday affair of marriage. Instead of new attitudes relegating morning dress to the rubbish-tip of outmoded clothing, first generation educated men, whose fathers probably married in government issue demob suits, now wish to mark the special day in a uniform that cannot even be called atavistic, as their ancestors, even as recently as Edwardian times, dressed in no such way, knowing that their betters had reserved such clothing exclusively for themselves.

For the upper classes it is distressing that their clothing – the togs of the nobs – can so easily be copied by the lower orders and become the dress of the yobs. The distinction of their fancy dress, which *did*, for them, have a basis in atavism, has been destroyed. They have to wait for coronations before they can assume a truly exclusive form of dress. Ridiculous as they look in their robes and coronets, and pathetic as those robes might be as tokens of power in the twentieth century, the aristocracy – unlike those who ape them – at least have the compensation of knowing that, by *making* themselves ludicrous, they also make their appearance unique.

Those privileged enough to have a close royal connection can, even in the 1990s, don dress which is absolutely exclusive to them. The Royal Orders each have their own old-fashioned uniform of mantle, hat and insignia to be worn with pride and little apparent sense of irony. This is pantomime dress, and as such perhaps fulfils a need. Unlike many nations, the British have never had a strongly decorative ethnic or peasant costume. Because of the stranglehold of our class system, only our aristocracy has been allowed the privilege of being gaudy. The tradition of the lower classes has been as watchers, impressed or thrilled by a pantomime they have never been asked to join. But it is a tragic performance. The pantomime is the British social system and the performance has gone on too long, continuing even today. The crowds who watch the modern performers, parading with their sovereign in Windsor, London or wherever, seem as unconscious as they do of the tragic, Toy-Town quality of it all.

Even more surprising are the troops – normally from the Brigade of Guards – who are present on these dressing-up occasions. If the members of the Garter, Bath and Thistle seem unaware that they represent the nursery area of Britain – dressed up in order to play games that will keep the people out of mischief whilst being not too noisy or disruptive of life beyond the nursery door – it seems impossible that the soldiers and their appearance do not give the game away.

Put a man in uniform and, no matter how irrational, monstrous or ludicrous his actions, he will be taken seriously. Who has not thrilled to the parade-ground antics of soldiers dressed in ceremonial uniforms? Fancy-dress military uniform makes even the silliest movements seem acceptable. It makes ceremonial wheeling around on a parade ground appear almost normal. It is even possible to imagine that it has some rationale. Actions are applauded which, if performed in sports coats and trousers, would be laughed to scorn. Scarlet coats, burnished helmets, bearskins and tight trousers move us once again out of the real world into that of the Toy-Town soldier – the chocolate soldier – of the nursery. And we are happy. We love ceremonial parades because they take us into a fantasy world of tradition. We are convinced that this world must be better than the realities of the present even if, on examination, much of it hardly existed 150 years ago.

The more obviously privileged world of upper-class self-indulgence – the champagne-and-strawberries life of pure Season pleasure, from Cowes to royal garden parties (where the Queen feels she can no longer afford to give her guests strawberries, despite her tax-free state subsidy to the tune of £7.9 million annually, guaranteed by us, the taxpayers, for the next ten years) – has been politically defused by the cleverest ruse of all in the class war. To make it seem harmless play-acting instead of the ruthless parade of privilege that it is, the Season has been manipulated, patronisingly enough, to appear a series of occasions especially for the ladies – opportunities for them to dress up and show off (Bless them!) whilst the yobs look on, envy and – it's only the ladies! – even laugh. This pantomime can please all tastes.

The Season is essentially the time for silly feminine hats. Bystanders might consider the male boater, topper and yachting cap more deeply disturbing as signifiers of a class so out of touch with its time that it should be heading for oblivion, but few laugh. Such headgear is seen, as male hats traditionally have been, as betokening rank and power. They are *not* to be laughed at. The hats of the ladies are a different matter. *They* betoken the empty-headed woolliness of a sex who wear them merely in order to look attractive, and are therefore immediately laughable, as all high fashion gestures are to those outside the world of high fashion. As if knowing their role without waiting to be ordered into it, women appear at Ascot, summer weddings and the like in hats that they know will have small boys pointing and roaring with mirth. They know, and they don't care. They are aware that it is the men who must have the dignity on these, and most other, occasions. The female part is to look pampered, expensive and erotic, as foolish as a flamingo and about as dignified as a kept woman.

They do not care, any more than their men folk, about the ill-bred comments of the yobs, because they view themselves as a super-species to whom all such remarks in matters of class, taste or social mores are simply irrelevant. The foolishly dressed upper-class woman may be well aware of the figure she cuts. It would be a mistake to assume that she is not as intellectually aware or acute in judgement as her male counterpart. But, like him, she has the confidence of a member of a ruling tribe with its own standards and values. That is why so many upper-class women turn their backs completely on fashion. They do not need to impress within their tribe, and do not care to entertain those outside it. They are like their men, whose attitudes were summed up in the doubtless apocryphal but nevertheless deadly accurate tale of the two dukes, one very much grander than the other, but both convinced of the social turpitude of those outside their narrow class.

Meeting in St James, the less-grand duke was so surprised at the shabby suit of his friend that he gently remonstrated. The other replied lightly: 'Nobody knows me here; it doesn't matter.' Two weeks later, the less-grand duke visited his friend at his country estate. The same shabby suit was worn and he again commented on it. 'Oh,' replied his friend, 'Everybody knows me here; it doesn't matter.' The story sums up the attitudes to dress of an inward-looking member of a tribe who has the confidence to assume that he is answerable to nobody but the members of the tribe – and not even all of them, at that. It is an attitude common to many self-satisfied and self-centred communities. The discreetly middle-class ladies of Mrs Gaskell's *Cranford* whose 'dress is very independent of fashion' held exactly the same view. It did not signify, however, that they dressed for exactly the same reason as the duke. With them it betokens mock modesty – 'Who would wish to notice *us*?' – whereas with him it springs from the same self-centred arrogance that in more overtly ruthless times produced the robber-baron, the pillager and the repressor of the poor. His indifference to his appearance is in reality an indifference to us, the outsiders from his class, who might, in our bourgeois insecurity, attempt through our clothing to suggest an image whereby we might gain society's approbation for our wealth and taste, and thereby dub ourselves that most despised creature of all – the *nouveau riche*, for whom no class has a good word.

Image projection has always been a major part of high-fashion clothing, and still is today. Despite our apparent greatly increased sophistication and our undoubted improved education, we still feel that anyone expensively dressed is to be admired as being, in an indefinable but positive way, not just a socially superior person, but better than the rest of us. Superiority was seen in the dress of the boss class. Sparkling white starched collars, well-brushed hats and gleaming boots were essential aspects of the dress of rulers. Gloves, worn as tight as possible, not only kept hands clean – they implied that manual work was not indulged in. Servants kept busy at copper and mangle ensured that their masters were always spotless, and barbers and hairdressers added the finishing touches, topping off the pristine edifice with just a hint of scent. Feeling grand, the toff would step out confident that, by appearance alone, he had distanced himself from his fellows – the toilers, sweaty, stained, essential but despised. The Victorians made their very morality a question of cleanliness, and we still subscribe to the view that nice people are clean people – and, even more problematically, that clean people are nicer than grubby ones.

Dirty bodies, dirty thoughts, low morals: thus ran the social sentence that condemned the poor for centuries. Of course, *nobody* was especially clean until well into the last century, and it was not until this century was comfortably advanced that Westerners could take for granted their *right* to be clean. As if to wash away the mental strain of generations of poverty, the working classes (and especially the immigrant classes in the United States of America), encouraged by advertising, saw the dawn of the new millennium as rising out of a cloud of soap bubbles. Cleanliness was no longer merely next to godliness – a concept never very practical for the poor and rapidly losing appeal for the workers in the early decades of the century; nor was it merely an essential staging post on the path to respectability – as it had been for over a hundred years. It had become the prerequisite for the sophisticated and fashionable life that beckoned so beguilingly from the cinema screen that it had even the poor and hopeless in thrall to the dreams it offered.

Jean Harlow . . . Joan Crawford . . . Bette Davis . . . Carole Lombard . . . the first ladies of the screen set the standard. American cinema fashion was squeaky-clean fashion. A hair out of place, or a button carelessly left undone, loomed large as social solecisms on the silver screen, literally and metaphorically drawing attention to the woman as slut. The same was true in England. From the Royal Family downwards, cleanliness was not just a state of being, but an intellectual attitude. Happiness, joy, sorrow, pain – cleanliness was an integral part of them all. Paradoxically, it was the editor of an American fashion magazine, Diana Vreeland – known in the fashion world as The Empress for the incontrovertibility of her *ex-cathedra* pronouncements – who summed up the depth of the situation when she said, apparently without irony, 'I love royalty; they are so clean.' It is precisely because film stars and royalty are so clean that they are admired.

In the thirties and forties, when cleanliness was still a struggle for many and a rare luxury for some, admiration turned to idolatry. Royal scandals, and even screen scandals, were treated very warily by the media because they knew that people did not want to be told that their idols had feet of clay. But, as the cleanliness gap has narrowed, so our view of actors and royals has modified. We no longer see them as necessarily better than us, and our curiosity about them is no longer motivated by hero worship. We look at the glamour and privilege of their lives and long for the worm in the bud to be revealed.

Queens of the screen or Queens of the Realm, the authority of cleanliness remains nevertheless undisputed. In effect, desire has become obsession, with bathrooms as fetish objects. Bodies barely dirtied are daily cleansed and anointed; clothes not soiled are changed as often. Is our obsession with cleanliness a neurosis, or is it merely another aspect of the effeteness of modern life? Urban living has brought mental stress and physical strain to increasing numbers of people, and their effect is surely all the stronger for the very limited range of emotions that society permits as outlets to 'civilised people'.

Sanitised values do not stop with our too-clean bodies and over-pristine dress. They are merely the outward and visible symptoms of a malaise. We have lost touch with the roots of humanity. City dwellers often complain that they are crammed on to public transport and confined to light- temperature- and air-controlled environments, that they feel like battery hens. But what makes us like those hens is our removal from the weft and warp of natural life. Children no longer hear the sounds of their mothers giving birth in the room next door. Babies arrive in sterilised hospital rooms. Young men and women no longer see grandparents being laid out and prepared for the grave on the kitchen table. They meet the coffin at the crematorium. The roots of joy and grief, so necessary to feed the psyche, are cut off in modern urban life, and in our search for emotional satisfaction we are left with nothing but trivia: new bathrooms, new kitchens, new cars and, the biggest sop of all, new clothes.

For centuries, life for most was village life, closed, intimate and aware. The idiot's moan, the suicide's cry, the scream of the butchered pig, kept us in touch with the depth and complexity of existence. Now we are left only with entertainment, indiscriminate and meaningless to the extent that starving refugees are viewed on our television screens with the same dispassion as quiz games, and the results of real motorway crashes cannot be distinguished from fictional representations of hospital emergency wards. We view life as an adjunct to ourselves. Narcissism is the rule of the age. Everything we do and see must be as clean and sterile as our persons.

Cleanliness creates a layer between us and the rest of humanity, in order to protect ourselves from each other. In broad class terms, clothing has long been used as a divisive tool, but now it also presents a barrier between individuals. Cleanliness of person and appearance has actually become an entity in its own right. No longer next to godliness, it is increasingly taking its place as the moral basis for middle-class life. The beauty parlour is its temple, the boutique its synagogue, wealth its sacred sacrament and its Holy Grail upper-class exclusivity. We are clean because our betters have always been so, and we look down on those who are not so clean as we are.

No wonder many young people have rebelled. They reject the clean approach as inhuman. They tear their jeans and buy scarred and ripped second-hand clothing. They emulate the rough manual worker whose jeans are working clothes, and the fighter whose combat gear or flying jacket have, it is hoped by those who purchase them from the surplus store, suffered the realities of weapons unloosed to kill. The young see the blandness of cleanliness – excessive, unnecessary cleanliness – as an obscene luxury bought at the expense of third-world people engrained with the filth and dust of a poverty and hopelessness that their elders assumed had been routed for ever from the West. They know that such distancing is as politically dangerous as it is morally repugnant.

The refusal to be dragooned into the urban cultural pattern began twenty years ago, but its roots go back much further. The popular theory that women's dress in the last century was cumbersome and constraining in order to keep them shackled to the house is largely nonsense. Except for the poor who, regardless of sex, had few freedoms, Victorian women were much more their own mistresses than we now care to imagine. In choice of dress, they were left to make their own decisions, albeit within proscriptions approved by both sexes. Those brave souls who attempted to introduce rational dress as an alternative to the cumbersome status clothes in vogue found that their enemies were as likely to be women as men. Whilst some women in intellectual and artistic circles took to it, the majority preferred to remain tied up with ribbons and bows as fashionable treats waiting to be unwrapped by men. The movement died still-born, aborted by ridicule.

It was in the early years of this century that Coco Chanel, ever perverse and keen to shock, decided that female fussiness was inappropriate for the new woman. Enjoying dressing up in her lover's clothes, she created her own shapes for women, based on items in men's wardrobes. Everyone knows the results. Chanel has been extravagantly praised as the founding mistress of modern clothing. Diana Vreeland said that Chanel invented the twentieth century for women – a statement as dramatic as it is empty, assuming as it does that fashion is the only reality for twentieth-century women. It is wise to recall the words of another, earlier and more thoughtful, editor of American *Vogue*, Edna Woolman Chase, who said that Chanel 'had the spirit of Till Eulenspiegel . . . one could never be sure whether her mischief making was deliberate or unconscious . . .'

Neither great creator like Patou, nor artist on the level of Vionnet, what Chanel had was flair, courage and, above all, personality. But what did she *really* want to make of women? Was she the first designer to laugh all the way to the bank? Anti-fashion of the sort that Chanel peddled has always had an appeal for women who are unsure of their intellectuality, nervous of their sexuality, and afraid of being manipulated through their dress. They reject what they see as the slave culture of the fashionable woman, who self-consciously dresses to reap the reward of male approbation. But few women, no matter how obsessed with their appearance, paid the inflated prices for *haute couture* clothes out of their own pockets. In a sense, it was the husband or lover settling the dressmaker's bills who was the true slave to fashion, forced to pay for, and approve, that which might well have not pleased, amused, or stimulated him.

It was the first generation college-educated young men and women who, in the seventies, belatedly followed Chanel's lead and turned their backs on crudely obvious status dressing. They went further. Their revolt into style cut across society's almost religious belief in the purity of cleanliness. Suddenly, it didn't matter if your jeans were stained, your boots down at heel and your body not automatically washed daily. Freedom was all that mattered – freedom from parental values, society's constraints and the need to conform; freedom to hold alternative views, drop out of college, reject the work ethic and take to a culture based on drugs. It was a movement of overwhelming intellectual arrogance, self-absorption and indifference to society. Furthermore, it was a movement of weakness, inability to cope with the world, and despair for the society that it ran away from. Inward-looking and self-absorbed, hippies, in Peter Carey's memorable phrase, 'had come to believe that jeans and dope and hair were a sign of some particular integrity' – and they were wrong.

To clothe such intellectual pretensions required an almost biblical simplicity. In dress terms, the movement saw itself as the offspring of religious cults. Long skirts, modestly patterned with tiny flowers, cheesecloth blouses and non-status beads for women, and embroidered shirts, velvet jeans and broad-brimmed hats for men had a new homesteader look to them (especially as the men were frequently wearing long hair and Old Testament beards) that seemed wholesome in its rejection of modern values. But, in fact, the dress proclaimed the essentially trivial nature of the movement. It was the pantomime stage again. Promising a new philosophy, all it delivered was localised irritation for police authorities. The whole back-to-nature hippy search for truth was, beneath the attitudinising, little more than a self-indulgent slap in the face of middle-class consumerism by people only able to deliver the blow because they had benefited from the very consumer society they rejected.

The chosen uniform – fancy dress of the most sterile kind – was taken up commercially and proved very successful. The firm of Laura Ashley traded on its pernicious fall-out for years. Much more important was the reaction to it. Punks, Hell's Angels and Rockers saw the inherent weakness in the clothes of the hippies: fantasy dress for a romantic

WELL-FORMED FELLOWS

In Renaissance Italy fashion was essentially ageist. Young men showed off their limbs while the mature man hid his under dignified robes.

A fashion that spread across Europe and lasted even into the present century was to dress your servant more magnificently than yourself in order to impress without being accused of personal vulgarity. Venice vied in magnificence with other Italian city states by allowing its gondoliers extravagantly beautiful clothing paid for from the city coffers.

PATRICIANS AND PLEBS

Dressing to impress, above and below the salt, always falls into a certain pattern.
The upper classes wear mess kit and white tie, diamonds and silk; the working classes
content themselves with the more mundane pearl button. Whereas the working class
show has almost disappeared, the upper class regalia of grandeur has not changed
since this photo was taken in 1931.

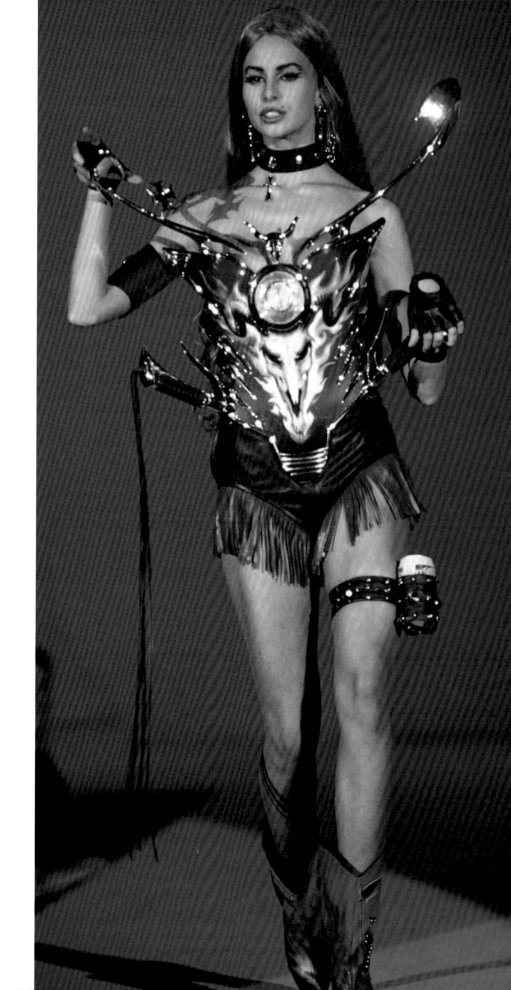

SAFE SEX

The pounding rhythm of
powerful machinery is often
equated with sexual
excitement. Men have long
assumed that the phallic thrust
of a car's bonnet or the
throbbing urgency of the
motorbike's roar present an
irresistible turn-on for women.
Norman Parkinson's picture of
a woman in a Molyneux gown
making love to the brute
machine is taken a stage
further by Thierry Mugler
who has the machine swallow
the woman up – or has she
swallowed it in her anxiety to
experience its masculine
strength? Both images tell
rather less about fashion than
they do about male fantasies.

rural existence as meaningless as it was banal. They knew that the future lay not with flower-filled meadows of organically fertilised grass, but on the garbage-piled streets, awash with the detritus of urban life.

Brutal, hard and uncompromising, punk style produced a fundamental fashion change based on an even more fundamental reassessment of humanity's position *vis-à-vis* the social forces that threaten it. Unlike the hippies – who ran away to Wonderland, just as the English upper classes and royalty have done – punks faced the facts of the future head-on. The importance of their dress cannot be overestimated and, indeed, has still not delivered its full impact. For an analogy of its long-term effect we must move from fashion to art. Punk brutality delivered a karate chop to fashion in much the way that Picasso, Picabia and Leger did to painting. It destroyed in order to reconstruct, and the new ideas it brought reduced the continuation of previous fashion styles to nothing more than decadent recycling.

Since the seventies, however, fashion has been consistently betrayed into this decadence by our desperate need for decorative deliciousness that demands no thought and presents no challenge. It is a need that refreshes itself from the same well as our need for royalty pageantry and upper-class dressing-up. Fashion in the last decade – that is, designer fashion, copied for our high streets – has been playing a game of ring a ring of roses, going round in circles, plagiarising past and present and refusing to turn terrified eyes to the future. True fashion has been stopped in its tracks for ten years, rooted to the spot in terror of what it has seen. If it follows historic precedent, it could be there for some time.

Victorian female dress betrayed the same sense of shock. The future of fashion was clearly expressed in the simplified dress of the Empire or Regency period, but society was not ready for it, and carried on playing decorative games and variations on an out-moded theme for the next hundred years. Not until the First World War did fashionable clothes drop the pretence and follow the path clearly indicated so long before.

Punks and hippies show humanity's various responses to its modern crisis – the horror of the moral impotence of the individual in the face of repugnant political develop-ments. The hippies decided to play decorative games in the way in which designers like Lacroix and Versace still do today, whereas the punks faced the brutal facts and began to dress for the ideological battleground ahead.

Punk approaches have not made outdated fashion design disappear any more than Picasso and his followers did with representational art. It has taken over seventy years for the public to realise that Picasso was right and that the thousands of more accessible, non-threatening and easily understood representational artists who took advantage of our fear of the new were wrong. The same thing will happen in fashion. 'Humankind cannot bear too much reality,' is endlessly restated in every facet of life, not least in the clothes we wear.

High fashion has largely been the history of fancy dress, of wearing clothing manifestly unsuited to the realities of life. It is so because fashion believers, like those in the plastic arts, respond badly to intellectual rigour. Just as Sir Alfred Munnings represents artistic woolly thinking compared with Ben Nicholson, so does Yves Saint Laurent in confrontation with what is being worn on the streets of London, Paris and New York. The indigent young wish their clothes to reflect the realities of their situation rather than the dream world of a designer cloistered and sequestered in Ottoman luxury, far from the pulse beat of the times.

The last twenty years have been cataclysmic for fashion. They have witnessed a complete shift in the nature of fashion power. No longer the prerogative of the rich, vain and under-occupied, it has become the province of the fit, healthy and young. They may also be rich, vain and under-occupied, but these are now secondary considerations. But all privilege is sinister, that of the young as much as any other. Just as those who live in the charmed circle of the upper classes have always managed to bewitch the rest into believing that such a circle can be justified in terms of continuity, values and tradition, so the music-loving, sports-crazed and healthy young have now beguiled us all into a St Vitus' dance that, for all but themselves, could prove the Dance of Death.

SIX

Protection and Projection

On 23 July 1987, the most monstrous question of the decade – even perhaps of the century – was asked by Mr Justice Caulfield. Summing up in the libel action Archer versus the *Star*, he urged the jury to remember Mary Archer in the witness box. 'Has she fragrance?' he demanded. 'Has she elegance? Would she have – without the strain of this trial, a radiance?'

The fact that Mr Justice Caulfield was not instantly sacked is worth some investigation.

Women have long complained that in the very way men compliment them, they insult. Beauty, even mere physical attractiveness, is taken as a measure of a woman's character, personality, competence and, indeed, her integrity. To judge a woman's worth in terms of her appearance is patronising – and it starts barely out of the cradle. 'Who's a pretty little thing?' is a question reserved for baby girls and pets. Boys are also indoctrinated into the role of their sex at an early age: 'Who's a big strong boy?' Girls are given the female role of looking pretty, whilst boys fulfil the male one of being strong. But not all girls are pretty, any more than all boys are big and strong. The result is a high proportion of adults of both sexes with inferiority complexes, inculcated almost from birth with the impossible demands of society – and it *is* society; women as well as men encourage the stereotypes.

Is it conceivable that Mr Justice Caulfield would have asked the jury to think of Jeffrey Archer in the same terms as he urged with his wife? Why then did he think of Mrs Archer in that way, apparently without causing offence to her or her husband? It is not merely that he was a foolish man, as judges so frequently are. It is that what begins in the cradle is unthinkingly kept alive by both sexes to the grave. Women expect compliments about their physical appearance. They enjoy them. Even my most active feminist friends are happy to respond positively to a compliment about their dress or hair. And why should they not? Where society has gone wrong is not necessarily in judging women by their appearance, but by failing to apply the same criteria to men. Had it done so, the judgement would not have been so narrow and looks would have taken their place alongside all of the other things that go to making up femininity, as a balanced part of the whole 'package'. Further, looks would have been part of the male 'package' also.

Two women can talk of a third in terms of her appearance – 'She looked lovely. Blue really suits her' – without raising any alarm. It is a measure of the strength of the sexual strait-jackets into which we have bound ourselves that neither women nor men wish to hear men talk in the same way. 'John looks really handsome with that moustache. And I love his green shirt. It really is his colour.' Such a male conversation overheard in a pub would have women blushing and strong men backing against the wall.

Why? What makes the sauce for the gander so unpalatable for the goose? Surely either both sexes should be able to talk in this way – or neither. Clothes make most people edgy because they can give away so many secrets, but that alone is no explanation for the paranoia that engulfs many men when dress is discussed. I have touched in an earlier chapter on the roots of this paranoia, which grew to such alarming proportions during the last century, in the male fear and loathing of homosexuality. This is something understood and accepted as the flaw of the sex. What matters more is the double standard that enables us to accept 'women's talk' as inferior to that of men. And we do so accept it – women included.

But there are signs of change. For generations, women have been the consuming sex: the shoppers, the seekers of the latest novelty. Whilst men worked – or smoked cigars in their club – women paraded the emporia. Victorian and Edwardian photographs show Oxford Street and Regent Street thronged with women, outnumbering men a dozen to one. Largely middle class, they had free time to fill and shopping, as was observed in a magazine at the turn of the century, was 'if done with diligence . . . so time-consuming'.

Through the course of this century, however, the greater leisure time of both sexes has been increasingly spent together. Segregation of pastimes into male and female has broken down at all age and class levels to such an extent that shopping, once the female privilege (or penance), is frequently a joint experience. In fact, it is the highlight of the week for many couples. We are all consumers now.

That alone, however, does not make us all confident of our judgement or taste. As manufacturers, retailers and designers realised in the late seventies, the boom in shopping had brought into their net vast numbers of people who were dyslexic in matters of taste and illiterate in terms of fashion. The skill of the informed fashion *aficionado*, parodied in the character of Cedric in Nancy Mitford's *Love in a Cold Climate*, was missing. The narrator, Fanny, tells how her mother 'brought me a little jacket in scarlet cloth from Schiaparelli. It seemed to me quite plain and uninteresting except for the label in its lining . . . I was wearing it . . . when Cedric happened to call, and the first thing he said was "Aha. So now we dress at Schiaparelli, I see! Whatever next?" "Cedric, how can you tell?" "My dear, one can always tell. Things have a signature . . . I can tell at a glance, literally a glance."'

It was because that skill, which requires effort and time to develop, was lacking among the shopping classes of the seventies that a visual guide was required. The designer label was born, along with the surge in advertising that made it effective. Fanny herself, being what Cedric described, not unkindly, as 'like the Royal Family, my darling. Whatever you wear you look exactly the same, just as they do', felt inadequate to the *couture* she wore. She was sure that, like her, others would not see the skill of her jacket and could only be impressed by the label: 'I longed to put this on the outside.' She was not alone.

In the mid-seventies, Italian designers were faced with an unprecedented consumer boom. Their countrymen, rich in lire, desperate to be smart middle-class consumers, but with little tradition in high fashion or sophisticated shopping, clamoured to be told the secrets of successful dressing.

Their cry was answered. A plethora of glossy fashion magazines appeared to fulfil their need, and they were read by all sections of the community, from the very young to those well into middle age. The age-old *passeggiata* changed its character. Instead of the traditional Italian walkabout in the cool of the evening, dedicated to nothing more demanding than gossip and flirtation, it became a fashion show. It was essential that Massimo had the right brand of jeans for the Saturday stroll – that is, the jeans featured in *Per Lui* – even if Mama had to be up at 5.00 a.m. scrubbing the *chiesa* steps to get the money – just as his girl-friend Concetta could be seen in nothing but the sandals she had fallen for in this month's edition of *Linea Italiana*.

Fashionable folk love uniform and must all wear the 'look' of the moment but, for these Italian fashion freaks, to do so was almost a matter of life and death. The first Saturday *passaggiata* of each month saw them in their droves wearing what the glossies had told them *must* be worn that month. As fashion's greatest conformists, they drew strength from seeing their insecurities dispelled by the almost identical clothes of their friends who sauntered to meet them. It was as if a wandering tribe, formless and without leaders, had found its saviour in the pages of the fashion magazines. Italian magazines were strong on editorial comment but that was nothing compared to the overwhelming amount of advertising they carried. At peak times (March and September), it outweighed editorial by four to one. More, it positively shrieked the 'right' names at the readers, from the grandest – Valentino and Lancetti, who vied to be first in the front advertising section – to the hundreds of lesser design firms that had sprung up like mushrooms in order to serve the boom.

It was advertisers who made the Italians (and subsequently the world) conscious of labels. They answered the pragmatism deep in the Italian soul. Why pay a fortune for Valentino jeans, if they look to the untrained eye exactly the same as a pair costing a quarter the price? The Italians are flaunters: if you've paid the money, they reason, let the world know. Wear the label on the *outside*. No wonder the joke said that a fashionable Italian made such a good read – at one time every item of fashionable clothing bore the label on the outside. The idea ran like wildfire through the fashion world and 'designer label' became such a cliché that, by the eighties, it had been reduced to 'designer', used indiscriminately as shorthand for something meant to be considered better than the average although, in reality, probably not. Now even that label has been discredited, as cheap copies of all the great names in fashion, luggage, watches and perfume have flooded the market.

They have done so because the Italians turned out to be just the tip of a particularly lucrative iceberg. The whole globe is in thrall to the snobbish world of the 'great' name. And, until the practice became *démodé*, vast numbers of people were willing to wear such a name on shoulder, breast, back of collar – anywhere it could be seen. Like all successful fashion, it was self-defeating. Fashion auto-destructs to make way for the new, and thus is always able to feed the need it creates. When everybody can wear a label, nobody wishes to any more. Names became too popular. They were vulgar and obvious – but what about logos? A new idea, backed up by a new word – no wonder it caught on. Wearing a crocodile, a polo player, a heraldic crest on your breast was much less desperate than carrying someone else's name. It was a more subtle way, almost an insider's way, of proclaiming taste, sophistication and, frequently enough, wealth.

Logos added the touch of class. Not only did they tend towards that unity that makes for conformity, confidence and assurance; for people who knew nothing about fashion and had not bothered to develop their taste, they also carried fashion authority. The fashion world is often accused of being fickle, when in fact it is no such thing. It is the opposite – totally predictable and reliable. Its well-spring – though rarely acknowledged – is snobbery, and always has been. For the person who cannot afford a Rolex watch or a Vuitton case, the snobbery of money is very important, and he circumvents it by accepting cunning copies; but real fashion snobbery has nothing to do with money. It has to do with class:

He opened for us two hulking cabinets which held his massed suits and dressing gowns and ties, and his shirts, piled like bricks in stacks a dozen high.

'I've got a man in England who buys me clothes. He sends over a selection of things at the beginning of each season, spring and fall.'

He took out a pile of shirts and began throwing them, one by one, before us, shirts of sheer linen and thick silk and fine flannel, which lost their folds as they fell and covered the table in many-coloured disarray . . .

Gatsby, in Scott Fitzgerald's novel *The Great Gatsby*, perfectly sums up the snobbery of male fashion in the twenties. He pretends lack of interest – so much so that he employs someone else to shop for him – but is unable to hide the pride he derives from his possessions. His attempt at upper-class indifference is spoilt by his need to display. He is a snob on both counts. he impresses with his taste – after all, *he* makes the final selection – but, because he is at heart a vulgarian, he cannot resist showing off his wealth. 'While we admired he brought more and the soft rich heap mounted higher.' It was Gatsbyism that had the new consumers by the tail in the eighties, making them determined to show, with varying degrees of subtlety, their 'class' – and, incidentally, their wealth. After all, with a few notable exceptions, the upper classes have not been noted for a lack of money to bolster that famous understated taste.

And, of course, if you have the taste and the social position, you can have fun impressing your peers. Again, literature best sums it up. In Isabel Colegate's *Statues in a Garden*, the upper-class beauty Cynthia Weston knows how to make an entrance:

And here she is in her black velvet and all her diamonds, pausing at the top of the stairs which lead, so conveniently for dramatic effect, down into the crowded reception room. And the faces turn, obediently . . . She begins to move . . . and she glides down the stairs with the velvet spreading out behind her . . . and she stretches out both jewelled hands . . . and what a benefit she bestows.

Although the novel is set in 1914, that is exactly the upper-class assurance that the benighted buyers of the eighties were trying to capture. But whereas Isabel Colegate's heroine simply *knew*, the eighties 'wannabe' simply did not. A Lagerfeld sleeve . . . an Yves Saint Laurent sleeve . . . a Bill Blass sleeve . . . they are all the same to fashion's yahoos.

If there was one fashion that brought more uniformity than any other during the eighties, it was what might be called Country House Clout. In a period when many people seem to have money, it is important for some, at least, to pretend to breeding. Ever since the TV adaptation of *Brideshead Revisited* that breeding has been shown by wearing country clothes, dateless, timeless and, ostensibly, anti-status. They are no such thing, of course. By not bothering to proclaim status, they suggest even more of that sought-after quality. Country-living clothes for urban lives proliferated. English classics like Burberry and Aquascutum were joined by new firms such as Next, who peddled the shooting-party style for people whose only experience of a dead pheasant was one pre-packed and cling-wrapped in a Waitrose cold cabinet.

The doyen of this socially convoluted uniform was the American designer Ralph Lauren, who lighted upon it in the mid-eighties, after several stylistically worrying forays into the American Homesteader and Wild West looks. With the declared intent to produce anti-fashion, Lauren looked to the past in order to clothe the present. He found his Valhalla in the sepia world of the American upper classes of the twenties and thirties. As a template for living in the eighties, he could hardly have focused on a less promising inspiration but, such is the power of the logo and the snobbery it pinpoints, the Lauren look soon had an enormous following. Its success was largely a marketing and advertising one, as there was virtually no new design input. Ralph Lauren's Rhinelander store in New York is his flagship. It is a triumph of goads and whispers, cajoling people into believing that the upper-class life of the past is available and appropriate for our times. So well judged is the wizardry, and so strong is our desire to ape our betters, that the ruse works. Polo-Ralph Lauren clothes have become a synonym for the class of those who wish to convince that they have far too much class to worry about being fashionable. By donning the dress of a moribund age, they have given Ralph Lauren, personally, the very way of life his clothes seem to promise them.

If the tweeds and watered silks of Ralph Lauren's uniform for yuppies are atavistic in their appeal, he is himself in thrall to the *true* uniform of the times. He wears jeans virtually permanently, including teaming them with black tie and tuxedo for evenings. Worn with cowboy boots, it is a look that posterity, even at its most charitable, will surely deem ill-advised. But the Lauren antennae are right. Jeans are the most powerful fashion uniform of the century. Americans have worn jeans in their off-duty moments – as in their hard working ones – for generations. Baggy and shapeless, they had seen the Americans through the thirties, forties and fifties, but they were not good enough for the Italians who, in their new craze for chic clothes for every minute and every activity of the day, were fashion's neo-Victorians. They it was who, in the late seventies, slimmed jeans down, sharpened them up and created what was in effect a completely new fashion garment. Like modern football shorts and those worn by Sir Stanley Matthews, the only common thread between traditional American jeans and their designer reincarnation was the material.

What is the universal appeal of jeans? Apart from their clearly articulated sexuality, why should they sell in more quantity than any other form of dress? The advance of fashion, as of much of civilisation, is motivated by mankind's protracted battle against boredom. No matter how suitable an item of clothing, no matter how ideal a concept, we eventually become weary and demand something else. This has not happened with jeans – and shows no sign of doing so. Most people have one pair, many have lots. In nearly all cases, they are the favourite in the wardrobe, reliable, friendly and trustworthy. More, they are undemanding. Denim is a material that can flatteringly clothe a wider variety of body shapes, whilst still delineating shape, than virtually any other. It is a material that can be put on and forgotten. Uniquely among high-fashion garments – and jeans *are* now considered high fashion – they can be worn without fear of damage and, even when skin-tight, without the discomfort and inconvenience so often associated with fashionable clothes.

They have more to offer. Unlike virtually all other fashion garments, jeans are dateless. They are never out of style because there is so little room for designer manoeuvres. There can be few other garments of which it can be said that an example bought ten years ago could be worn today and appear as fashionable as a pair bought yesterday. Eschewing flairs, gathers and stone-washing, classic jeans are always fashionable and yet, paradoxically, do not have the in-built obsolescence that fashion garments always possess.

Fashion is about belonging and not belonging. Wearing Gucci loafers proclaims you a member of a group. The man who uses a Zippo lighter or a Mont Blanc pen signals that he is outside the huge body of those who use throwaway lighters and ball-point pens. The strength of jeans is that, though universally worn, they remain attractive to the fashion-conscious élite. And, of course, unlike most fashion items, there is no particular reason to 'rip them off'. The fashion *cognoscenti* believe they can tell the difference between Levis, Pepe and Easy (although as they are all conveniently and prominently named there is no need to) and for the rest of us it doesn't really matter.

So runs the received wisdom, but it is quite untrue. Label snobbery and loyalty run as high in jeans as in any designer clothes. They may be mass-marketed and sell in their millions, but we still feel that *our* brand is the only one that counts – and we replace it year after year with more of the same. This level of brand loyalty is rare in fashion, where designers and labels tend to have their day and then slip into a more or less permanent limbo. Jeans buyers are as fanatically hooked on 'their' make as people are on washing powders, toothpaste or brands of coffee. Jeans, you might say, are for life – the Coca-Cola of the fashion world.

Fashion, along with music and dancing, has become a major hobby for teenagers. They are *the* label freaks of the nineties and it is in trainers rather than jeans that their prejudices and preferences show – 'Trainers are the most important thing in my life!' Manufacturers battle for the lead in this most lucrative of markets, knowing that the label of the moment will swoop ahead of all others, no matter how good the competition. Manufacturers are also aware of how volatile the teenage market is. If everyone is wearing Nike this month, it can be guaranteed that they will all want Reebok, or a new Nike design, next month. There is a hysteria about the teenage world of style that makes adult fashion freaks, even at their most intense, seem truly laid back. Teenagers are the people who have actually lived up to the fashion cliché that a style is to die for. Scorn for someone who cannot afford the top ranges of trainers – costing well over £100 per pair – has led to suicide. Determination to have the best has resulted in a considerable increase in thefts from sports shops, as well as muggings and even, it is rumoured, killings.

Fashion feeds on frailty. Teenagers are, almost by definition, insecure. They gain strength from conformity. They wish to be part of a group, sporting a common identity. They make the ideal fashion victims. The trainer war is the first all-out onslaught on their sensibilities. It exploits their desire to belong as well as their need for heroes. It is also part of a bigger battle initiated by television and capitalised on by newspapers: the battle to turn us all into passive sports followers to such a degree that sport becomes the central prop of our culture. In many respects that lamentable situation was reached long ago with our two 'national' games, football and cricket. But television has widened the net to include athletics, swimming, horsemanship and even snooker as placebos against the realities of the world. The spin-off has been twofold: sport has been employed by a manipulative and exploitative area of mass marketing, whilst making increasing numbers of people passive recipients of second-hand experience.

Passive or no, the recipients, especially the young, insist upon wearing the gear of the active athletic warrior. This desire was given a great fillip in the early eighties when breakdancing became a youth cult. The baggy tracksuits, hooded tops and, above all, fancy trainers of the breakdancer bridged the gap between music, dancing and athletics. It was a lead that manufacturers later exploited when they realised that, although an athletics star could swing many thousands of teenagers behind him if he endorsed a popular brand, his effects were minor compared with those achieved by a pop star of the calibre of Madonna, who merely had to be seen wearing a brand in public for sales to rocket. LA Gear named its trainers after Michael Jackson's hits 'Billie Jean' and 'Speed Demon', and paid the pop star a hefty commission to do so. MC Hammer was brought in by British Knights in order to boost their sales. These endorsements betray what trainers are really for: sitting around and fighting boredom through music or videos. They are a manifestation of sportswear's fall from grace into mere leisurewear. Just as 'designer' tracksuits by Fila or Ellesse are not always sullied by sweat, these trainers do not often pound the athletics track.

Aware of their awesome influence on teenage minds, some trainers' manufacturers are using their power to attempt to manipulate the behaviour of their customers for the good. Advertisements have dropped the anti-social urban warrior image and replaced it with suggestions that, for example, Nike Air Jordans' wearers don't drop out of school and don't take drugs. It might be one of the few genuine examples of fashion having a conscience but, if it is, it is as well to remember that it is the conscience of the rich. We all know how that differs from normality.

Whatever the advertisements proclaim, the teenage trainer mania has a sinister side. It has deftly hooked the very young into the commercial fashion scene and made them the most vulnerable and responsive of buyers. Trainer freaks see their worth and strength as so intertwined with their footwear ('Wearing Nike gives you *power*, man') that they hang on to their brand of trainers as a comfort blanket against the harshness of the world. The trainer bonanza could be the first distant trumpet of a new social order – an order that makes clothing and its nuances more important than they have been since Victorian times and more political than in the Tudor period.

Of course, all fashion change occurs in response to manipulation, but it has rarely been politicised. What can be foreseen with the teenage fashion hysteria is the dissemination of political and cultural messages through clothing and its presentation. Perhaps in the next century, Big Brother will not merely be watching us; he will be clothing us too. Dress can be used to manipulate attitudes. We have only to think again of Ralph Lauren's huge success to realise how it happens. Lauren wishes to do nothing more sinister than make a great deal of money by clothing people's dreams and aspirations, but he does this by creating a look for them to conform to, and too much conformity endangers democracy. Every dictator knows this. Rigid dress conformity already rules large sections of the teenage world and it can be manipulated for cultural and social purposes. Harnessed to political aims, fashion would be so powerful that it could deliver dramatic results. Already we have seen the power of the dress of disaffection in the Hippies, Punks and Goths who see their clothes as part of their ideology. How easy it would be to use dress to create attitudes (as opposed to its traditional role of exemplifying them) in the way that the Hitler Youth Movement did in the thirties – especially in such an intense and fanatical world as that of the teenage fashion freak.

Uniform of any kind speaks with a forked tongue. It can menace, or it can comfort. Always, it betokens authority. Part of the reason Mr Justice Caulfield gets away with asking outrageous questions is the way he dresses. His legal garb is meant to cow. Were he to make such remarks whilst wearing jeans and a sweatshirt – or even a plain grey suit – he would be laughed out of court, or pelted with rotten tomatoes. He knows that and so do all of his fellows in the law courts of the world. Their dress is a form of protective clothing. It deflects the arrows of common sense as effectively as a Crusader's armour did the Saracen's shaft. As a nineteenth-century writer pointed out, 'dignity cannot embody itself with little things, hence the custom of wearing large wigs.' Despite the many law reforms of this century, judges still sit wearing an outfit that not only has no links with the reality of today, but also psychologically transports us back to the eighteenth century when they had the power of life and death over the miscreant. It is hard for them to say goodbye to such absolutism – as their clinging to the outdated dress of a vanished power makes clear.

When a judge dresses, he is donning a carapace against us but, more, he is setting out to intimidate, psychologically, morally and physically. We must look at him and go back to the days when we grovelled, powerless, before his omnipotence, afraid to say yes or no; terrified even to look up. His robes and wig protected him from our dissent and made him as distant from the humdrum everyday world as an Inca God. They still do today. The fault lies as much with us as with the judge. His appearance continues to awaken ancestral terrors of such magnitude that we allow him to speak in a way both ridiculous and dangerous. We actually crave the power he has over us. We want him to make decisions – and we need his outrageous dress to act as an excuse for our need. Looking at him, we feel that we cannot stand up against such a powerful figure, carrying the weight of centuries of judgement. It is comforting to switch a problem to his curly-wigged head, so reminiscent of that of a sheep.

The garments of the judge have been retained quite consciously as a means of control. They are helped to be so not merely by their antiquity, but also by their colour. Black denotes finality – the cap of the death-sentence, the garb of the undertaker, as well as the pronouncement from the pulpit – but it also represents reliability, sobriety and, above all, authority. Clothes and their colours have no meanings in themselves. We impose a meaning on them because we look at them not with an innocent but with an experienced eye, one conditioned to draw certain conclusions from what it sees. Our minds react to visual stimuli conditioned by previous experience, either our own or that of others. We know that politically powerful men wear suits. We respond to the suit as part – even proof – of their power. We do not expect men in Hawaiian shirts and shorts to wield the same sort of power. We only accept that they might do so after we have seen enough of them wielding power in their suits. We acknowledge that George Bush dressed for fishing is still a man of power. So strong is the memory of his suited figure that he loses no credibility when wearing something else. When a man wears black, he assumes in our eyes a gravitas that says 'Take notice of what this man is doing and saying, for you may be in trouble if you do not,' because the experience of generations is that black is worn by people in authority, who might well be prepared to bully us mentally and physically in order to impose it. Black, therefore, becomes the colour of fear, impersonal and all-consuming.

That is why it evolved as the colour of death. Always a cultural presence, through disease, childbirth, riding accidents and the cruelly short lifespan of peasants, death reached its apogee in the nineteenth century. Under Victoria's tearful guidance, it became a central cultural force in Great Britain. Or, rather, its trappings did. So elaborate was the etiquette of death that the appearance of mourning became more important than the mourning itself. The sting of death was removed, subsumed in a plethora of ritualistic details of which none was more important than dress. Grief could not be hidden; it had to be paraded as a personal indulgence imposed on one's fellows, who were eager to partake in the sorrow in the most sentimental way possible. This projection was not just a form of grief therapy, but also a display of pride. The bereaved was elevated to a position above the common herd by a society that morbidly fed on the finality of death.

Naturally, in an era of masculine arrogance and female sensibility, when *Woman's World* could point out in 1889 that 'the inferior always expresses grief for the superior', the brunt of mourning fell on the woman, and the word widow was as noble for women as the male word hero. Naturally, too, in an era when she had clothes to pass her time but not much else, the joy of mourning for many a woman was in dressing the part. Crape became the material of death, beloved for its propriety and, above all, its opacity. In a period when 'shiny' materials such as satin and silk were prized by fashion as betokening light, movement and gaiety, crape, which had no reflective qualities, was a reminder to all that cruel darkness, stillness and grief had visited the wearer. It absorbed the light in a highly satisfactory way. Its drabness was prized as producing the 'deepest' mourning. The darker and flatter the dress material, the greater the grief and the higher the approbation of society. As Dickens wrote in *Dombey and Son* of Mrs Pipchin, who wore widow's weeds for over forty years, her black bombazine was 'of such a lustreless, deep, dead, sombre shade, that gas itself couldn't light her up after dark, and her presence was a quencher to any number of candles.' The worldly Trollope realised even more that clothing could substitute for grief in this most mannered world. The Duchess of Omnium in *The Prime Minister* described a widow as not shedding tears, but pointed out that 'her gown, and her cap and her strings were weeping.'

For many a woman, glad to be rid of a tyrannical husband, widowhood was possibly a pleasing prospect and her widow's weeds were worn as a smokescreen to hide her true emotions. They were a lengthy camouflage. John Morley, in *Death, Heaven and the Victorians*, quotes *The Queen* of 1880 writing about the intricate etiquette of mourning dress, which was as tightly regulated as a military uniform, and from which only the foolish or the bohemian would dream of straying. The more rigidly controlled, the more uncomfortable and the more constraining a widow's dress, he points out, the greater the glory of grief. Crape was worn for a year, after which it could be replaced by 'widow's silk', a flat, non-reflective material which was still to be heavily trimmed with crape. Only after twenty-one months could crape be finally discarded, and it was two years from the date of death before a widow could wear half-mourning. Even then, black was the pride of her wardrobe, discreetly joined by violet, lavender, mauve or grey. Caution was demanded whilst walking the social tightrope of death. Mrs FitzAdam 'as bold as a lion . . . rustling in black silk' scandalised the inhabitants of Cranford who agreed with Miss Jenkins that, so soon after her husband's death, 'bombazine would have showed a deeper sense of her loss.'

For men, the raven sex, mourning was hardly an issue. By mid-century they already spent most of their waking hours dressed in black. At no time did they look sleeker or more elegant than in the evening, when their clothing, which was normally limited in any scope for individual variation, became a rigidly applied uniform. A contrast of deep black and sharp white, the evening dress of the upper middle-class Victorian male was the perfect clothing for a sex sufficiently arrogant – or wise – to have divorced itself from the need to express its personality through individual decorative variations. Here was a uniform which said 'I am superior, as is all of my sex. I do not need to vie with my fellows. Our individual worth is shown by our differing intellectual, political and financial wisdom – and that is the only variation that matters.' By adopting such a stereotype, men were implying that their time was far too valuable to be squandered on something so trivial as dress – much better to leave all of that 'nonsense' to the second sex, and one's tailor.

But, of course, it was far more complicated than that. The rationale behind developments in dress is rarely codified or, perhaps, understood at the moment. It is only the perspective of time that enables us to fit together the pieces of the social jigsaw that illuminate and exemplify the complicated processes at work – the cultural, moral, intellectual and financial well-springs of society's actions. Men banded together to create a strong sex. Unity brings strength and, by doing so, protects the weakness of the individual by the camouflage of that collective strength. Uniform always brings confidence. So does exclusivity. The lure of a club is not that it says 'come' to the masses. What use would that be? The strength of any club – from Whites to the Freemasons – is that it says 'keep out' to the vast majority of people. It is significant that clubs that are so exclusive are so beloved of men, whereas women's clubs – the Women's Institute, the Countrywoman's Guild – open their arms to all. What the Victorian male effectively did was to make his whole sex a club. Women – the weaker sex – were shut out and men showed it by their uniform club dress, exclusive to them.

As the nineteenth century progressed and moved into the twentieth, men increasingly gained individual strength from uniformity of dress. The concept of power dressing developed. It was an entirely male concept and it reduced virtually all men's clothing to a uniform, tightly controlled by upper middle-class usage. Black for evening – elegant, no fuss, uncompetitive and yet making a statement about the superiority of the sex – was joined by dark grey and deep blue for the day. And so it has remained.

Real power in the twentieth century is financial. Even political power bows before it. Any man who deals with money acknowledges that power – and his devotion to it – by wearing sombre clothing that impresses on the world the seriousness of the stuff. Bankers dress almost identically to clerics in sober dark suiting highlighted with white – just like male evening dress – in order to show, as the evening dress does, that the individual is less important than the concept, be it God, Mammon or masculinity. The traditional dark suit of the middle-class male – 'the dress of the puritan man of business who sees no justification for any human activity but financial success' in Gill's words – is 'counting-house clothing'. But it is more. It is the ritualistic robing of a sex that has sacrificed everything on the altar of power.

So powerful has been the mass message that we all believe it. We need our men of decision to dress in sober suiting just as much as we need our judges to wear wigs. Who would trust a bank manager wearing jeans and a coloured vest? Who would patronise an accountant in shorts and a T-shirt? We have been so well indoctrinated that we actually believe that the dress makes the man, and we expect those who deal with money – most sacred of commodities – to dress with the sobriety of a cathedral dean.

Boss-class dressing, proclaiming the man who must be obeyed, is a bedrock of political success. Flamboyant deviation is allowed to only the most extrovert of characters. For every Disraeli, who got away with something akin to fancy dress, there are hundreds of Gladstones, who believe wholeheartedly in the rectitude of unimaginative clothing.

E. Moers in *The Dandy* describes Disraeli wearing a black velvet coat with satin lining, purple trousers with gold seaming, a scarlet waistcoat, lace ruffles and masses of jewellery. Gladstone, on the other hand, was appalled to see rowers in Oxford crossing the High in shorts. He felt that between river and college, trousers should have been worn. It was his narrow attitude that won the day.

It is no coincidence that in the 1980s, when money became the god not merely of the City but also of vast numbers of people, the sober dark suit again became so important in politics. We have always wanted our politicians to dress as bankers – which shows how deep is our misplaced confidence in the men who misuse our money. The correct dress for Parliament is sober and, until the advent of socialist MPs, was exclusively boss-class. Frock coats and toppers were *de rigueur*. When Keir Hardie entered the Palace of Westminster as a new socialist MP he caused a sensation by appearing in a working man's suit and soft hat. The effect was rather as if Neil Kinnock had walked into the House wearing a tracksuit and trainers. So-called gentlemen in the Shires amused themselves by sending top hats to Hardie and suggesting that their tailors might provide him with a frock coat. With the strength of his conviction, he rose above all the ribaldry. Nevertheless, he pinpointed the socialist dilemma. Men in political power make us uneasy if they do not dress to that power. Socialist MPs on television, wearing safari suits and sandals, did not capture the confidence of viewers used to seeing their Conservative counterparts in tightly waisted pin-striped suits and club ties. On the principle that 'if you can't beat 'em, join 'em', Neil Kinnock in the eighties, when trying to revamp his party and boost its flagging fortunes, revealingly enough called in a fashion PR firm to advise on where they were going wrong. In no time at all, socialist MPs were dressed in boss-class clothes; the curling collars, twisted ties and strangely cut suits which had previously characterised them were a thing of the past. They conformed so closely to the traditional image of an MP that they appeared indistinguishable from their Tory counterparts.

Even women have been forced to conform to sobriety in order to be taken seriously in the market place. The saddest sight of Threadneedle Street is the deadening similarity of the 'City types': men of all ages wearing identical dark suits. From the back, they are like a vast funeral cortège. From the front, many now sport a bold tie or an outrageously striped shirt – permitted for their links with school colours, rugby shirts and college blazers – but these are allowed only to men. Women pay for their entry into the club by attempting to make themselves as much like traditional bankers as possible. In a pale version of the Victorian white and black statement (strong in its original arrogant confidence) they conform with a half-hearted grey and cream or navy and white uniform which in its compromise shows a lack of the very confidence that the *un*compromising male statement makes abundantly clear. These women are not to be obeyed. They are handmaidens only in the priestly devotions of man and Mammon.

Pathetic as their lot is, it is far from unique. Wherever a woman wishes to penetrate a traditional male enclave, the price extracted is the denial of female garb. In the Inns of Court, women, overawed by the power of the law, dress in black – not the chic little black dress with the discreet pearl necklace but the surrogate suit. Even if they could, they would not wish to wear fashionable, colourful dress. The reason is clear. By doing so they would put themselves into an arena where taste functions. If you question a person's taste in dress, you are likely to question judgement in other fields. The law, like the world of money, functions through mystique and the willing suspension of disbelief. Allow the modern world to penetrate too deeply and the privilege of the power is exploded in the light of commonsense. Questions must then be asked: is the stockmarket, with its jittery swings from euphoria to despair, in the right hands? Does its very volatility suggest that it is run by immature, hysterical men who overreact in the most childish way? Does the law of the land benefit by being in the hands of the likes of Mr Justice Caulfield? As the people in power well know, dress is a disguise. We rip it away at our peril.

FIND THE LADY

The archetypal fashion figures, for most of this century, have been stick-thin. Many of the world's top models have had the shape of an adolescent boy, but they have always attempted to look lady-like and aloofly elegant. That has now changed and many designers like to see their creations shown in as crude a way as possible. Paradoxically, it is in drag clubs that the full feminine figure is still admired and attempts to keep alive 'lady-like' glamour are still made.

THE GOLDEN TRIANGLE

The silhouette of the hunter – triangular and streamlined through hard physical effort – has been the male ideal for centuries. Robert Devereux, Earl of Essex, relied on his tailor to provide the attributes of masculine power by padding his shoulders and cinching his waist. Modern man turns to the gym and works the remedial treatment on the flesh itself. In either case, the results are a body shape singularly unsuitable for urban man.

UNDERCOVER STORY

Eighteenth century perfection of line was achieved at a cost. Comfort and ease of movement were sacrificed in order to elevate and project the bust and narrow the shape of the bodice. This corset required 162 pieces of whale bone to underpin the effect seen in the stomacher embroidered with multicoloured silk flowers.

THE LADY AND THE TRAMP

Coco Chanel believed in the dignity of women and felt that, to have any integrity, female fashion should be a logical part of a woman's life. She disapproved of excess and believed in a minimum of decoration. Under Lagerfeld, the excess at Chanel has reached epidemic proportions. Is his success a reflection of how women really wish to dress in the last decade of what has been their most liberating century, or are they victims of a highly sophisticated 'hype'?

FORM AND FREEDOM

The late twentieth century
fashion ideal is the fit, healthy
body of youth, carrying no
excess weight and firmly
toned. The fact that women
continue to believe the
designers and the magazine
editors who suggest this is
an interesting proof of how
easily education, experience
and social sophistication can
be undermined by
psychological warfare.

SEVEN

Fashionable Politics

All clothes are political. When British *Vogue* features a linen dress by Christian Dior at £5,500 it is, in a land where the government pays an unemployed single man £41.40 a week, making a political statement. When a PR person avers that a blouse is 'competitively' priced at £185 in London, a city where large numbers of the country's 2,700 registered homeless are sleeping on the streets, that is a political statement. When an editor of British *Vogue*, asked about the cost of designer clothes, replies 'You cannot ask the editor of "Vogue" about prices,' that is also a political statement.

The cost of fashionable dress is obscene. Narcissism and vanity have always made the rich spend on their backs amounts that would keep their retainers – quite apart from the peasants without the gates – comfortably for months. Diana de Marly, in an *Antiquaries Journal* article on fashionable suppliers of clothing between 1660 and 1700, makes the point that, when the 3rd Earl of Sussex had a suit and cloak costing £23. 6s. 6d. made in 1664, a footman was earning £4 per year. The clothes of the rich often cost, as she says, 'more than the ordinary person earned . . . in his whole lifetime'. In 1673, the Duchess of Lauderdale and her daughter ran up clothing bills of £227. Even a hundred years later, a working-class family of seven or eight would rarely have an annual bill of £5 for clothing – and frequently it would be half that amount.

No Western governments have ever had the courage to redress the balance between rich and poor. Regardless of political colour, they shy away from taxing the rich and their profits at a level of stringency which would assure that they could not afford self-indulgence in dress. Not even the most hedonistic, vain and self-involved woman, to take a modern example, can *justify* spending close on £30,000 on a beaded *couture* evening dress – to be worn once, twice, rarely more than three times. That this amount of money *is* spent is an indictment of how we control and organise the flow of wealth. In an ordered world, such sums should not be available for dress.

The conscience of the rich is more flexible than that of the rest of us, and ways have always been found to take the sting out of the parade of wealth. As early as the eighteenth century, grand houses were thrown open so that their treasures could be ogled by suitably decent persons who would appreciate the honour bestowed and not attempt to steal the silver. Middle-class visitors, permitted a promenade in the ducal gardens, could be trusted not to repay the privilege by carving their initials on a tree trunk or scrawling messages on the folly walls. Their glimpse of the aristocratic life was granted on the assumption that they would behave themselves and play by their hosts' rules.

A conscience – even one belonging to a rich man – needs to be salved. Charity has always been part of the aristocratic hold over the other classes: gardens opened for the middle class, bowls of gruel for the poor. It has always been self-congratulatory – 'we must care for the less fortunate' – and superstitious – 'we are so lucky'. Privilege must be paid for. Even the stupidest persons know that, if you take a great deal out, it is only expedient to put something back in. The charity ball is the ideal way to have your privileged cake and eat it. The sting of wearing a dress that cost enough to keep an unemployed man for over a year is, it is assumed, removed if you are paying through the nose for an indifferent meal and caterers' champagne, and gambling large amounts for useless tombola prizes, all in the name of charity.

Charity events – to raise funds for the local church, comforts for the lads fighting the foe, or to help the chronically sick – have an honourable history. Village-based, they traditionally took in a broad cross-section of the community, all of whom felt that they were 'doing their bit' for the cause. The fête, the social evening, the public dance gave everyone the opportunity to wear their finery with pride, whilst avoiding the *sin* of pride due to the goodness of the cause. However, in this century, the situation has changed. Dressing-up for charity has become the preserve of the rich and privileged, who clearly echo C. Willett Cunnington's remark that 'To be charitable is more virtuous than to be taxed, and costs less.'

Charity balls became the rage during the twenties, when unemployment and its social evils were so gapingly apparent that they could not be ignored. The impetus came from America, where rich society needed, as all society does, something around which to form. Lacking the natural European focal point – a royal family – people who had become startlingly wealthy through banking, railroads, mining or whatever, organised their social scene around charity. It has developed into a multi-million dollar seasonal indulgence, raising money for anything from anti-drug organisations to art galleries and minority groups. In London there are at least two charity balls a week and, in the winter, several, with frequently more than one a night. On any night, the cost of the dresses, hairdressing, make-up and jewellery far outweighs the amount raised for charity.

Although, of course, funds are raised in many ways other than balls, what is outstanding is how middle-class the recipients are. The top charities in the Charity Aid Foundation's annual lists show only a slight yearly variation. The National Trust, Imperial Cancer Research, RNLI and Oxfam are always in the top eight, along with Guide Dogs for the Blind, Dr Barnardo's and the Salvation Army. Even in the post-Aids world, charity is deeply traditional and, with the exception of Oxfam, extremely chauvinist.

What the assumptions of the editor of British *Vogue* and the organisers of charity balls ignore is the fact that consumerism cannot be compartmentalised. An outrageous act of vanity in one section must be related to costs in other sections. The Dior dress does not stand in a vacuum. Giving £1,000 to the Save the Children Fund is a generous, if self-preservational, gesture, but it pales when we remember that the person making the gesture is wearing ten times that amount in dress and jewellery.

Fashionable dress has always been costly. In the past, the cost was considered part of the apparently immutable equation that society should be unbalanced, with control vested in a few very wealthy people who lived lives quite separate and different from the vast majority. The difference between the rich and the poor was so great that it was accepted, much as the poverty of the Third World is today, as something too overwhelming to tackle. But it *was* tackled and the gap has narrowed. Even the last decade, which saw the gap widen again under a British prime minister and an American president as apparently indifferent as Stalin to the needs of the hapless, helpless and hopeless, has not entirely altered the modern equation. The very rich and the very poor are fewer than they were even in the last century, though there remain too many of both.

146

The Paris designer is such an archetype that it is difficult to remember that he has had a comparatively short reign. His Age of Absolutism covers little more than 150 years, since he arose to meet a new and specific clothing need that developed in the nineteenth century. As the middle classes marched forward on paths of increasing prosperity, they required the sort of clothing that proclaimed that prosperity. Until then, fashion change had been initiated by the twittering classes – the courtiers who filled idle lives by falling into a passion over the colour of a Queen's ribbons, the cut of a favourite's sleeve, or the shade of a dauphin's stools. Dressmakers were an important part of that world, but their role was largely to take instruction, not dispense it. With rare exceptions, they were treated as extensions of the servant class. Aristocratic taste was too informed and confident to admit any prompting from those of a lower social class.

The nineteenth-century middle classes were a different matter. Conscious of their *nouveau riche* status and frightened of making social *faux pas*, they lacked the confidence of the aristocrat. They were desperate to be told – how to dress, how to walk, how to enjoy their newly bought status. Trusted shops and emporia answered the need until, in 1858, one of their employees took the quantum leap and became a *couturier*.

The life of Charles Frederick Worth is well-enough known. Born in Lincolnshire in 1825 to a drunken father and feckless mother, he was apprenticed to a local printer at the age of twelve. He hated it and, at the age of thirteen, took up an apprenticeship with the London store Swan and Edgar. In 1845 he moved to Paris, and two years later was working for the city's most fashionable drapers, Gagelin and Opigez. He was there for twelve years before setting up on his own with Otto Bobergh, a fellow salesman. His wife was as ambitious as he, and worked hard at her social contacts to find a patron who would wear her husband's gowns in the right places. She persuaded Princess Metternich, the wife of the Austrian ambassador, to order two outfits. Wearing one to court, the Princess caught the eye of the fashion-conscious Empress Eugénie, who began to order clothes from Worth. Such approval from the royal leader of fashion meant that Worth was instantly taken up by the fashionable. When Worth became the Imperial dressmaker his success was assured, and the world flooded to his establishment in the rue de la Paix.

Single-handedly Worth changed the social balance between customer and purveyor of clothing. The despised dressmaker was gone. High fashion required a dictator who would show how much he scorned his clients for their lack of fashion culture. By treating them abominably and over-charging them disgracefully, Worth ensured the lasting success of the breed he had brought into existence.

Worth's arrogance was endlessly satirised. Under the pseudonym 'La Vicomtesse des Trois Étoiles', a journalist described how great ladies waited patiently in rows like lackeys in his antechamber until he deigned to see them. The report continued, 'That is power, that is real autocracy. Ladies may be allowed to put on arrogant airs . . . but to reach the man who possesses the magic formula of their elegance and beauty they have to leave their arrogance in the anteroom, or at least the cash desk.'

Hippolyte Taine describes Worth lounging in a velvet jacket with a huge cigar, and asking a customer, 'Madame . . . who has recommended me to you? In order to be dressed by me you have to be introduced. I am an artist with the tone scale of a Delacroix. I compose, and a *toilette* is just as good as a picture.' Condemned for treating duchesses disdainfully, almost with 'unparalleled rudeness', Worth's approach was summed up by a reporter: 'At a single glance he recognises the fault with a dress: "With her waist, Madame must wear only draped material. It is too *décolleté*. Let the material lie diagonally across the shoulders. The spray on the corsage is far too big."' His customers loved all this flummery – or, at least, were prepared to accept it – because they loved the effect their appearance in a Worth creation always provoked.

True kings had long since ceased to rule even fashionable circles. The power of courts had been swept away. Instead, fashion now produced its own kings. Unelected and unanswerable, they were more absolute than any monarch would have dared to be. Edicts and proclamations daily issued from their lips; personal feelings were wounded; snubs and rejections cut across the normal rules of society with an outrageous disregard for rank. Late Victorian and Edwardian *couturiers* were so grand that their behaviour seems laughable to us – the antics of impossibly puffed-up nonentities – but in their time their rule was total. Led by Worth and Poiret, the *couturier* had, by the beginning of the First World War, become the arbiter not merely of dress, but of all the social niceties of the fashionable urban world.

It was in this period that a split developed in the upper classes. Many English aristocrats turned their backs on smart city life and abandoned fashion as bourgeois and *arriviste*. They returned to their estates and led their lives in tweed as tough and immutable as the gorse of their grouse moors. Others, in love with the idea of a fashionable king – Edward VII and his clothes-conscious queen, Alexandra – were happy to become exotic coat hangers displaying the genius of their *couturier* at the plethora of social occasions developed for that pleasure. Stuck in their murky 'seats' in the sodden Shires, the sort of aristocrats portrayed by P.G. Wodehouse glowered at the monkey attitudes of the Mayfair fashionables whose behaviour so interested Lorelei in Anita Loos's *Gentlemen Prefer Blondes*, a yawning chasm between them both.

The gap has never been fully bridged. Even today, a large number of aristocrats consider an interest in fashion to be a sign of vulgarity. They would faint dead away at the cost of most designer labels. They flick through *Tatler*, appalled at the antics of Reggie's nephew or Sybil's eldest girl, and shudder with distaste at 'ladies' who pose for fashion shots in *Harper's and Queen*. They buy fashionable clothes only for weddings and functions at St James's or Buckingham Palace – and even then would hope to get away with something run up by the gillie's wife or a little dressmaker in Cirencester, topped off by a Simone Mirman hat.

Despite such attitudes, and even though he fell from his heady pinnacle of Edwardian times, the *couturier* maintained absolute power over every aspect of fashionable dress and appearance until the rise of ready-to-wear after the Second World War. But by the mid-1960s it seemed as though his time was gone. The hegemony of Paris as the centre of fashion was successfully challenged and overthrown, initially by London, then Milan and, finally but most significantly, New York. The greatest consumer nation in the world had learnt to produce its own high fashion during the war, and by the late sixties American fashion was a sophisticated and well-developed business. The fashion map had been permanently redrawn. Not unlike the shrinking pink of the British Empire, the power of Paris as a world force was dramatically reduced, season by season.

Paris was losing clout, but this weakened neither the power of fashion, nor the arrogance and grandeur of its purveyors. The days when Worth could make a duchess wait for weeks before allowing her into his presence are long gone. They will not return. But inflated egos seem an essential part of the fashion world, and designers of ready-to-wear, despite the humble end of many of their clothes, expect to be treated as great artists. Indeed, one of the more extraordinary developments of the last decade is the way in which designers, who should be basic, practical men, again transformed themselves into old-style *couturiers*, worthy of fear and sure of a taste beyond question. By doing so, they turned the fashion world of the eighties into something not far removed from the Belle Epoch, with which the decade shared what James Pope-Hennessy immortalised as 'that delicious atmosphere of sumptuous second-rate'.

The bizarre lust for grandeur has struck Italian and American designers most forcibly, even though their countries are nominally dedicated to egalitarian societies – Italy having abandoned the concept of a hereditary aristocracy along with the monarchy in 1946, and America never having had one. This does not stop their designers enjoying an almost regal life style. Designer A in Italy demands that his cohorts arrange for the lift to be always open and ready for him in any hotel or restaurant he might visit; designer B in Italy telephones from his chauffeur-driven car to his atelier five minutes before his arrival so that all staff can be lined up ready to witness his progress to his private office; designer C in America insists that white flowers be placed in every room through which he passes; designer D in America makes it an offence rating instant dismissal if anyone enters his studio when he is with a client; designer E in Italy forces his London PR to fly weekly to Milan for a twenty-five-minute meeting, the time and day of which are never allowed to vary. The list of pomposities, idiocies, blatant misuses of power and ostentatious consumption of money goes on and on.

No wonder that fashion designers live their lives on this plane of pride and prejudice. They are creators of the trappings of class distinction, and, as such, are important cogs in the turning wheel that ensures that the wealthy and privileged feel superior to the rest. That is not remarkable. What is worthy of wonderment is that so many people still wish to follow their decadence.

A woman who went to Worth in the last century paid an extremely high price for the honour of being dressed by the world's greatest *couturier*. The customer at Balenciaga in the fifties paid for one evening dress more than a boiler-maker earned in a year. *Couture* is not cheap. Exclusive and delicate materials are always costly. Handwork takes time and, as Benjamin Franklin pointed out, time is money. But it was not merely the pocket of the *couture* customer that suffered. Made-to-measure clothing demands a considerable dedication of time if it is to be executed perfectly. In the final flowering of true *couture* – the era of Dior, Balenciaga and Fath in Paris; Hartnell, Amies and Stiebel in London; and Norrell and Mainbocher in New York – a woman who dressed in *couture* had to spend at least two months a season being fitted for her clothes. The result was a dress of a perfection hard to imagine today. Quite apart from design, cut was vital. Balenciaga was said to have spent a lifetime chasing the Holy Grail of the perfectly set-in sleeve. Taste also was crucial. Understated and underplayed, each *couturier* had his own level, as recognisable to the *cognoscenti* as a building by Wren or Inigo Jones to an architectural student. Again, it was said of Balenciaga that, when he was asked how much taste a customer required, he replied 'None at all. I provide that. She provides the body.'

It was a rarefied, privileged and indulgent world – perhaps even a rather foolish one – but it worked to the highest principles and disciplines of art. That is why old *couture* is so popular with collectors today. They are buying dressmaking and tailoring at their peak, as historic and unrepeatable as a Grinling Gibbons carving or a Huet tapestry for Aubusson. Paradoxically, private customers are buying these clothes to wear. It is ironic that clothes owing their whole *raison d'être* to the fact that they were created to fit perfectly and precisely one unique figure – that for which they were made – should now be sought after and worn by people who destroy the point of *couture* by wearing clothes that cannot fit them without alteration. It is the equivalent of lopping a few inches off the Gibbons' carving or Huet tapestry to fit them into a given space, and shows a total lack of understanding of the *essence* of *couture*, which it reduces to the level of mere pretty frocks.

Modern *couture* cuts corners. Not all work is done by hand. Nevertheless, prices are still high. Almost as high, and much harder to justify, is the cost of ready-to-wear designer clothing. Like anyone else pandering to vanity, dress designers expect to make money, and they always have. Worth became spectacularly wealthy; Poiret, although he died a pauper, had amassed a fortune before his life took its downward spiral into personal debt; Dior and Balenciaga were more than ordinarily rich. However, their potential for money making had limits. Working in *couture* and producing one-off dresses made money, but it also cost money. Perfumes and licensing agreements were not the huge money-spinners they are now. What marks the modern dress designers out from the *couturiers* of the past is the almost unbelievable amount of money they amass in a matter of some ten or fifteen years of trading.

Calvin Klein, Ralph Lauren, Giorgio Armani, Pierre Cardin, Yves Saint Laurent – these men have enough company and personal wealth to be able to bail out governments if they wished to. They are a dramatic and extreme personification of the modern idea of worth. They amass money not solely from greed, nor for the exercise of power (although they can, and do, exercise it) but from necessity. In the modern fashion world, the parameters of worth are proscribed by the amount of money made and, if it comes, success cannot be tempered or controlled. The designer is either not quite a success (as is the case with most British ones) or so much so that his profits go galloping away. Once he has 'made it', people who buy his clothes are psychologically convinced that they are buying into his worth. By wearing Calvin Klein jeans you make a little part of the Klein miracle your own. Further, by wearing his label, you assure that you will also be successful – albeit on a less spectacular scale.

'Dress for success' books, colour consultants and make-over specialists all miss this point. Their advice about colour, style, pattern and shape is irrelevant because they ignore the real key to success in the modern world. That key is the willing self-deception of a philosophy that believes that, by wearing a 'top' label, the individual will be lifted to the same heights by its talismanic power. The belief goes further: pay more money for the label than your bank manager and common sense can countenance and your chances of success are even more enhanced. As long as you are wearing Armani, you will behave as you feel an Armani wearer should behave – coolly, with an understated elegance and authority. You assume, subconsciously, that everyone who matters to you will also know that you are wearing Armani and will allow you to partake of the magic aura that surrounds his genius.

Modern designers are richer than their predecessors could have ever dreamed possible. Their success breeds increased sales – and further success. They have become household names in a number and range of households unimaginable to Patou, Schiaparelli and earlier designers. This does not just happen by selling clothes. In fact, it is hardly through selling clothes at all. For every woman who can afford an Yves Saint Laurent suit, there are hundreds who, because of the lure of that unattainable suit, force themselves to afford his perfume, or a scarf, or some jewellery, even a pair of tights. Anything in order to be hooked up to the life-giving name.

Designers make huge profits from their licences, especially those for perfume and make-up. They could reduce the retail price of a £200 scarf to fifty pounds, and still be in profit. A ready-to-wear suit at over £1,000 cost less than half of that to make; sold at £500 it would still make money. The reason that designers do not reduce their prices is not primarily greed – although that is a major element in the fashion world. It is that they know of our need for exclusivity – which we almost invariably see in terms of money paid through the nose and, more important, money that others cannot pay. If Ralph

Lauren clothes were as cheap as those in Next, who would want Ralph Lauren?

In the early eighties, the heady boom period of the designer label, prices were pushed through the ceiling in what can only be described as luxury rag-trade racketeering. The right label, carefully marketed and advertised, backed with fashion editorial support, could command virtually any price a quixotic designer and his cunning accountant cared to snatch out of the air. Nervous customers were informed that the high costs of designer clothes were justified because this was investment dressing – a heady phrase for the upwardly mobile.

The public fell for the concept, flattered by the link between their taste and style and the 'old money' connotations of investment in traditional upper-class areas such as fine furniture, pictures and silver. The message was simple: investment dressing was a 'class' approach to clothes. To bolster the illusion, retail outlets were also given the 'old money' feel. Following the style set by Ralph Lauren, clothes shops were suddenly all mahogany and brass, reminiscent of venerable banking halls, long-established art dealers or even Edwardian private yachts. Of *course* clothes bought in such surroundings were a good investment. You could almost *smell* the security of old money.

It was all a confidence trick. The styles might well be timeless and able to be worn with confidence for years to come, but the designers neglected one vital ingredient. The purchase of a Shaker chair or a Sheraton sofa is an investment because, quite apart from their beauty, they have quality. They were made to last. But in fashion, quality was the essential element to which designers gave scant thought. The investment fell apart and sagged, victim, often enough, of third-world tailoring deficiencies. Hems, badly machine-sewn; poor quality thread; skimpy seams that split open; cheap interlining – or even none at all – meant that these highly expensive clothes had no longer life than others with a price tag considerably lower.

Once prices have been pushed up and are accepted as the norm, the damage is done. They never drop. Similarly, all the shoddy workmanship in the world cannot besmirch a designer's name made desirable by sophisticated advertising and editorial presentation.

The successful dictator knows that to have the bodies and possessions of the people to whom he lays claim is not enough. He can settle for nothing less than their souls. Only when he has those can he command total obedience. A fashion dictator knows it also. It is popular to deny the modern designer the absolute autocracy of his predecessors, but it is wrong. The modern designer is still a dictator. All that has changed is what he dictates. We are all in thrall – not to the width of his collars, length of his skirts or depth of his *décolleté*, but to his name and what it stands for.

The fashion pyramid is built on snobbery – ours, as well as the designer's. It is held together by gullibility – ours, not his. We *want* to believe that great labels represent high quality, as they did in the past. We refuse to accept the evidence of our own eyes. Only after buying the £400 blouse that seems so convincingly silky do we read the tag that reveals that, despite the top designer name, we have bought a synthetic material. We continue to buy the designer sweat shirt rather than the Marks and Spencer one, even though we know from bitter experience that the former will shrink and its colour run while the latter, at a fraction of the cost, will behave itself. Not even in Victorian times has social life been such a game of status, and the most valuable chip for many is the name of a designer – as important as the right address, the prestigious make of car and the smart holiday hotel.

It is made valuable by advertisements – frequently for products other than clothes, to which the designer has lent his name – and by fashion journalists who, by persistent reiteration, can make even the most arcane designer names sufficiently common for chat-show and soap-opera audiences to recognise them. The effects of such familiarity on high-street, non-designer clothing are real, but difficult to quantify. Designers for mass-market labels rarely create their lines under the sole influence of one big-name designer. Their collections are an amalgam of what they see as the best and most commercial ideas of the season. The days when one designer could instantly set the tone for all the others – as Christian Dior did with his New Look – are gone. The fashion world is now too big and too varied to be dominated in that way.

This scale is one of its major problems. There are too many designers vying for attention. They produce too many ideas – and too many of those ideas are derivative, second-hand and commercially meaningless. To excuse this embarrassing trend, fashion apologists have created the concept of post-Modernism in dress, where there are no rules or canons of taste and decorative devices from any period or style may be mixed with impunity. It surfaced towards the end of the eighties, a decade of increasing desperation in fashion as world economics took their toll of high retail profits. It was ingenious but meaningless, very like the concept of 'style', created earlier in the decade as the ideal cover for fashion uncertainty: unquantifiable and indefinable in any meaningful sense.

The term post-Modernism first was coined to cover an eclectic style explosion in architecture which, after the plainness of Modernist building – to many, barren and banal – reinstated decorative detailing. It was essentially a retrogressive movement and it took architecture back to the mid-Victorians. As a *new* architectural approach, it was doomed, because no new technology had been advanced to create a radical new way of constructing buildings. Instead, post-Modernism subjected architecture to cosmetics, interested only in surfaces. Like plastic surgery, it changed nothing fundamentally. The same flaw lies at the heart of fashion post-Modernism. The way clothes are made has hardly altered in the last fifty years, give or take a certain technological brisking up here and there. Man-made fibres such as Lycra have been developed and exploited but, otherwise, technical advance has been almost nil.

It is possible to say – without too much wriggling – that fashion *has* its modernists. Courrèges, Cardin and, most notably, Chanel all believed in a minimalist approach that eschewed applied decoration as far as possible. Zoran, Alaïa and Donna Karan have followed in their footsteps. But it has been impossible for them to create a movement. That is because fashion is no longer linear as it was in the fifties, flowing from salon consensus to street acceptance. It is now lateral, based on fiercely different enclaves that have little connection with each other. What could be less similar than the designs of Gianni Versace and Romeo Gigli, Jean Muir and Vivienne Westwood, Hubert de Givenchy and Jean-Paul Gaultier? Yet each one thinks of himself as an Italian, London or Paris designer.

Even if we accept that post-Modernism relates to nothing more radical than the use of decorative detail, then fashion has been post-modern for the last 400 years. Its modernist period would have to be the draped purity of Greek and Roman robes, and the simple linearity of early medieval dress as, since then, decorative adornment has been the norm. The concept becomes meaningless. What modern fashion *does* have in common with architectural post-Modernism is the eclectic plundering of the past in a search for decorative *trompe l'œil* to disguise how little fundamental fashion change there has been. Old copies of *Vogue* and *L'Officiel* are anxiously pored over by designers increasingly desperate to keep up the flow of ideas. They feed on the prodigality of peers and predecessors alike.

Fashion has a fecundity that rivals that of nature. As in nature, much of the seed is spilled on the ground and comes to nothing. Most top designers produce too many collections. With their main women's and men's lines, cheaper versions of them for a separate label, possibly children's wear, household goods and accessories, they are often responsible for thousands of ideas each season via their design teams, whose role is to realise concepts that might have been carefully planned by the maestro, sketched hastily on an envelope, or merely communicated verbally. Many designers also produce collections for other houses. In addition to his own-name line, Lagerfeld, for example, designs for Chanel in Paris and Fendi in Rome. Clearly, with these sorts of commitments, a designer becomes more a businessman, organising, channelling and leading the design potential of his employees, than the creative artist he was in the past, able to keep personal control over everything in his house.

All designers produce collections that are too large. There are often sound, if hidden, reasons for doing so. Fabric manufacturers, who may be anonymously subsidising the designer with cut-price materials, help in show and advertising costs or, less obviously merely by talking to the 'right' people. They do so for the publicity their materials obtain by appearing in the show. Their eyes are set not on the retail public but on the trade – the people sitting on the buyers' and business side of the catwalk. They are the ones who, seeing a fabric used by a top Milan or Paris designer, might be inclined to buy it for their own up-market ranges. Fashion commentators rarely mention fabrics, patterns and trims; their interest is in a designer's line. Within the trade, however, that is the least interesting thing. Huge shows are not merely for the benefit of the journalists. They also parade the up-to-date development in the nuts and bolts of fashion, from the latest surfaces and colours to the newest ways with leather, jewellery and, of course, make-up which, along with hair, is especially created for the show so that the new season's colours achieve the maximum publicity.

All of this is not to deny the invaluable publicity work done by journalists, who are so efficient at 'pushing' names that they are often seen by designers as an extension of their PR machinery. A fashion editor who goes to the fashion shows held in Paris, London, Milan and New York twice a year will have the opportunity to see as many as eight shows per day, every day including Sunday for a period stretching over two months in twelve, and will, in one year, be exposed to more than 30,000 outfits. Each of these outfits will contain at least two ideas: the overall fashion statement that the designer is making that season, and an additional one dealing with decorative details and variations. In the case of many designers, there will be a plethora of ideas fighting for attention in every outfit, and even the most professional fashion editor will be hard-put to notice, let alone remember, all of them. Accessories will also be bursting with new ideas. When nothing can appear to be a re-run of last season, everything must change. Only novelty gets coverage.

Does the fashion industry need such prodigality? Is there any logic in designers tossing off ideas that are never used? The answer, of course, is no. Customers are not so fickle that they want every item of clothing to be changed each season. Even mass manufacturers, who will often pick up the details that go unnoticed or discounted by others, simply cannot assimilate all the available ideas. The fashion industry has spawned a multi-headed Hydra which is out of control. It has done so in a neurotic over-response to one of the most basic of human characteristics.

Curiosity – the desire to know what comes next – is what keeps fashion change rolling. Like children shaking a kaleidoscope to create a new pattern from existing components, so fashion followers open a fashion magazine with a feeling of desire. It is a desire for something new, although the components are as unchanging as the human figure for which clothes are created. An armhole is only such if an arm can go through it. A collar placed where the neck cannot take it is no longer a collar but a gratuitous piece of decoration: beguiling, amusing, shocking or exciting as may be but, finally, meaningless as a collar.

The seventies were a difficult and confused decade in the aftermath of a fashion upheaval. The sixties' mini, although brief-lived, had a profound influence on fashion in that it made established designers insecure. Suddenly, Paris seemed in danger of becoming irrelevant. The mini had nothing to do with the *couturiers'* perfumed halls, and did not wish to. It was an iconoclastic fashion which, if not actually born on the streets, took all its inspiration from them. Worse, the streets were not even the boulevards of Paris. Whether or not the first mini was created by Mary Quant (popular favourite), André Courrèges (most likely contender) or Pierre Cardin (pretender to the crown), it soon became apparent that traditional fashion approaches had no place in its continuance and that what mattered was what happened on the streets of London. When dresses were so cheap that they could be bought one Saturday and discarded the next, novelty, not quality, was at a premium. Fashion's teeny-boppers gobbled up ideas at an alarming rate and still yelled for more. They did not care about good value. What mattered was that the new dress was different from the one worn last week. Such an attitude was a blow to the heart of traditional *couture*, an industry based on painstaking, costly and time-consuming techniques aimed at perfection of cut, fit and finish. It was as if the doors of the Athenaeum had been burst open by Millwall Supporters' Club.

The designers of the mini boxed themselves into a corner, and their very success contained within it the seeds of their downfall. By making the mini the *only* fashion (so powerful that it even had to be worn, in modified form and with disastrous results, by the royal family at the investiture of the Prince of Wales in 1969), Swinging London had limited any new statement to mere decorative detailing until, inevitably, boredom set in. Although the mini had equalled the huge success of Dior's New Look of 1947 (although not beginning with such a dramatically uncompromising début that made every other designer's clothes *instantly* old fashioned) it had less staying power, because its shape and size were too limited a canvas for designer variations.

The evolution of a fashion resembles a failed love affair. Overwhelming desire eventually turns to disenchantment and then the determination to find something new. The demise of the miniskirt precipitated a desperate search for something new. Length, volume, scale, colour, pattern: everything changed, not over a period of several seasons, as traditionally, but almost every season. By the end of the seventies, traditional fashion sources were so exhausted by the demand for constant novelty that the only way forward seemed to be through a renewed iconoclasm of a severity that made the ruthlessness with which the mini had pushed aside all other styles seem almost benign.

London post-punk student fashion tried once again to assert that fashion originality came from the streets. Although not without influence, the premise did not convince, and the true impetus for short-term fashion change – which, in this case, turned out to be fashion regulation – came from an unexpected quarter. Following the lead of Kenzo and Issey Miyake, who had been in Paris for some time, young Japanese designers brought their ideas to the traditional home of fashion. Misaligned and illogical to Western eyes, their clothes at first appeared casual. In fact they were very formal, and calculated to be worn with all the self-consciousness of theatrical costumes. They caused such a furore that they unwittingly diverted the path of fashion sideways, away from the progressive logic of punk and up the sterile cul-de-sac that believed that decoration was a substitute for the logic of fashion change.

Japanese fashion, with the exception of Miyake's, seemed so uncompromising and strange, so ruthlessly ageist – relying for its effects on the figures, faces and movement of extreme youth – that it frightened Paris into an appraisal of how it could fight back. What did it have that made it unique? The answer was its traditional decorative skills. So desperate were the non-Japanese designers that they looked back to the heyday of *couture* for new inspiration. If it seems extraordinary that the approaches of the fifties could be seen as the saviour of the eighties, that is as nothing compared to the incomprehensible fact that the designers were correct. The tired old conventions of a form of dressmaking with no social relevance to the modern world were revived, misused and misunderstood. A new sub-*couture* fashion movement was born.

In the vanguard, waving a particularly garish flag, marched a new designer, Christian Lacroix. As house designer for the old-established firm of Patou, he was given his head to revamp the *couture* line, apparently with no stylistic or financial restrictions. Lacroix took his opportunity with both hands, producing endless pastiches and vulgarisations of the clothes designed by Dior, Fath and Balenciaga in the fifties. For the first time, humour was introduced to high fashion. Whereas 'amusing' beach and resort wear were well known, and young fashion had often had a grin on its face, serious clothes had always been *serious*. Diana Vreeland was right to point out that no great *couturier* ever set out to amuse. We might look back with modern eyes to the clothes created by Schiaparelli when she worked with Dali and was deeply under the spell of Surrealism and find them amusing; but this simply is to misunderstand the woman and the movement. Surrealism set out to shock. It was an art conceived to startle art lovers out of a bourgeois desire for things actually to be what they seemed. So with Schiaparelli. Her famous ripped dress and hood of the late thirties was meant to alert us to the dark march of Fascism across Europe – how easily the dress could have been torn on barbed wire or ripped with bayonets – whilst recalling the medieval penitent with his slashed cloak – the sackcloth and ashes mortification of the flesh. It was a peculiarly apt commentary on the late thirties, when refugees and unemployed gazed accusingly at the rich enjoying the luxury and safety of their wealth. On a more prosaic level, Schiaparelli's ripped dress was shocking in its visual juxtaposition of a luxury fabric – silk – and apparently wanton and vicious destruction. She seemed to be pointing out the transitory and self-indulgent nature of high fashion, even, perhaps, its insensitivity to the realities of the troubled thirties. However such clothes are read, they cannot be considered amusing, any more than can the early work of Rei Kawakuba and Yohji Yamamoto in the eighties.

Politics and fashion make uneasy bedfellows. Radical political philosophies normally attack bourgeois complacency and conformity. By its very nature fashion is bourgeois. The only way to use it as a political tool is to destroy it and reduce it to rags. This is what Schiaparelli and the early-eighties' Japanese designers did, in a highly decorative and stylised way. Whether such figurative gestures can have any political meaning is debatable. Ultimately they might signify no more than Valentino's slick and shallow response to the Gulf War, for which he produced a glamorously slinky evening dress embroidered with the word 'Peace' in several languages. It was a sick joke on the level of Zandra Rhodes's misuse of punk's torn and pinned garments in the late seventies. Taking the imagery of poverty and hopelessness and re-creating it in an expensive and glamorous form is as insensitive as it is patronising. Using a dress designed for the most luxurious and self-indulgent of occasions to make a comment on the horror and privations of war is offensive in its opportunism. Both are examples of the designer using politics as a decorative diversion, not meant to change attitudes, but merely to amuse. It is an approach to fashion and politics demeaning to both, and yet guaranteeing coverage in the world's fashion press.

Amusing and newsworthy as Schiaparelli's mutton chop- and shoe-hats might seem, they were created not to make us laugh but to jolt us out of our visual complacency and predictability, out of our belief that objects can have only one use and significance, out of our world of petty bourgeois realities and into the free world of dreams and illusions. Hadn't Lautreamont, the poet of Surrealism, pointed out that incompatibility brought its own beauty, like 'the chance encounter of a sewing machine and an umbrella on an operating table'? It is wilfully to misunderstand Surrealism and to belittle Schiaparelli's intellect to assume that her clothes inspired by the movement were meant to do anything as transitory as amuse. Good art, major or minor, sets out to shock and to change attitudes. It is never content merely to make us laugh.

Christian Lacroix appears to understand none of this. To fashion purists and feminists alike, his work at Patou and later under his own name, is insulting both to clothes and to women. His lead was followed by Karl Lagerfeld, who has also created clothes to make us laugh – at women as well as their dress. Both he and Lacroix were able to produce *faux couture* because, despite the delighted squeals of fashion's more gullible journalists that the new era of *couture* was upon us, there was, in fact, no serious eighties' revival of *couture* dressing. Costs and time kept customers scarce. But there was a huge revival of interest in *couture-style* clothes. Most of the major Paris houses gave increasing time and budgets to *couture* collections. Several followed the lead of Dior and brought in designers, at vast expense, to create the most extravagant *couture* collections ever seen. 'Newsworthy' was the buzz word, because this new *couture* was created mainly for publicity.

Although the lure of the top names took the fashion trade by surprise in the eighties, the fragrance manufacturers were ready. Designers were not the only ones to give their names to perfumes: fashion 'personalities' like Paloma Picasso and stars such as Sophia Loren did the same. There was even a scent associated with the heiress Gloria Vanderbilt. Traditional *couture* houses (the originators of designer scents) realised that they must fight back. They did so with the one glamour weapon exclusive to them: *couture* clothes. Extravagantly beautiful clothes with a heavy bias in favour of spectacular ball gowns were created largely to please photographers, stylists and art editors. The old adage that the only good dress was the bought dress was virtually rewritten. Now the only good dress was the one that photographed magnificently for the fashion magazines and kept the name of the house prominent in their pages.

Faux couture is in many ways a magnificent exercise in futility. The number of dresses bought by private customers is minuscule. The number able to be worn anywhere but on a catwalk is not high. These are clothes to be looked at, and very little more. Their main value will be for future historians, who will surely gaze amazed at what the great designers felt appropriate for post-feminist dressing. The new *couture* shows us how they would dress their 'ideal' woman when freed of all commercial, social and practical trammels, and it is a chilling and ultimately sterile vision. Even more worrying is the way in which some women appear to applaud their chauvinism.

As it could be said that New York society is based on the daytime and the 'ladies who lunch', so London society is of the night and the ladies who dance. New York fashionables spend money on daywear – the chic suit, the well-cut dress; their London counterparts buy ball gowns. One of the more pernicious effects of the revival of *couture* as a source of fashion ideas – the toxic fall out from the Lacroix-Lagerfeld axis – is that it has encouraged London's plethora of small-time dressmakers, trading as *couturiers*, to produce ball gowns which are not merely impractical and inelegant, but betray a complete lack of understanding of what it is the new *couture* is making a pastiche of.

The American hippie movement was anti-materialistic. It could only flourish in a highly supportive capitalist society like that of North America because, as an essentially non-productive movement, it required money that it could not generate itself. The movement was a dream, literally and metaphorically. The New York designer, Christian Francis Roth faces the facts of modern economic life by swathing his model in dollars.

THE IDEALISED IMAGE
(previous page)

No woman ever looked as impossibly elegant as Barbara Goalen. She was unique among models during the fifties in that her persona was infinitely more important than most of the clothes she wore. Women did not think in terms of looking stunning in Dior or Balenciaga. What they had in mind was looking like Goalen, no matter whose clothes they were wearing. She was the trail blazer in the movement that made model girls the carriers of female dreams just as film stars had been in the thirties.

LADIES AND GENTLEMEN

When Vesta Tilley performed before Queen Mary in a Royal Command Performance in 1912, the Queen averted her gaze throughout the whole act because she thought a woman in trousers was the height of indecency. Actresses like Dietrich and Katharine Hepburn, whose appeal was often sexually ambivalent, made trousers an acceptable fashion for women in everyday life. In the seventies and early eighties, Giorgio Armani brought the look to perfection - as could be expected from a man who began his designing life in menswear. The look still has great appeal as this shot from Ralph Lauren's show for Spring 1992 makes clear.

THE AGONY AND THE ECSTASY

The figure bound and constrained is a powerful aphrodisiac in the world of Sado-Masochism. The bondage of tight corsetry has been a feature of pornographic dress for men and women for centuries. What is interesting, as the twentieth draws to a close, is how fashion magazines present the woman constrained as a sexually exciting image for *women*.

ADAPTING TO REALITY

In love with youth, contemporary fashion has increasingly created clothes impossible for anyone over the age of thirty to wear with confidence. In the affluent eighties when the young had big money and small commitments there was no problem, but in the harsher nineties things have changed. The young no longer have sufficient money to endlessly renew their wardrobes and the successful woman in her thirties or forties can find no high fashion that she wishes to wear. The balance between creativity and universality has been destroyed. That is why variations on the Chanel suit have enjoyed such a revival. As the picture shows, it could be worn by the less than perfect figure and still be acceptable.

FEAR OF FOLLOWERS
(overleaf)

Like dictators, pop stars need to be protected. They have to be kept apart from the supporters who give them their power. Michael Jackson is flanked by guards to keep his fans away, very much as an absolutist South American head of state might be. The similarity does not end there. Jackson's dress – jacket frogged in traditional military style and dark glasses – needs only a peaked cap to make the comparison perfect. But the feet – and the rebel's white socks – give away the fact that Jackson's power is not political but emotional. Without the posse of policemen, he could literally be torn apart by adoring fans, who follow him as uncritically as any dictator's supporters might.

Even at their most vulgar, Lacroix and Lagerfeld know precisely the elements of fifties' *couture* that they are satirising. They understand the symbiosis between line, fabric and scale; they are aware of the necessity for balance between movement and proportion in even the most extravagant of ball gowns; they realise the *structure* of a garment. In other words, they know the nature of *couture*. They understand even as they desecrate. Their London equivalents destroy the tenets of great *couture* simply from ignorance – not only theirs, but their customers' too. Futile as the life of the *couture* customer of the past may have been, it was a life informed in the business of dressmaking. Client and *couturier* were partners in knowledge. That is why fifties' *couture* will remain the benchmark for the twentieth-century dressmaker's skills, whereas eighties' couture will eventually be seen as little more than a 'prop' from which the photographer creates his own minor work of art, just one part of a stage set alongside lighting and all the paraphernalia of his craft.

Fashionable dress must have its 'stage' upon which to perform. In the past, when fashion was a pleasure confined to the upper classes, the stage was a private one, the performance was given behind closed doors and the audience and the performers were one and the same. It was the world of private balls and functions open only to those in the know, the *cognoscenti* who could appreciate the care, thought and money lavished on appearance. The participants wore clothes for making an 'entrance'. Because the entrance was made under critical and informed eyes, the clothes had to be right: spectacular but not vulgar, memorable but never ostentatious. It is a world now vanished. In the words of Diana Vreeland, 'There are no clothes for making an "entrance" now because there are no rooms left for making entrances. What we have now are "drop dead" clothes, and they are not the same thing at all.' She was speaking as a fashion purist and unconsciously echoing the words of Beau Brummell, possibly the greatest purist of them all, who nearly 200 years ago, pinpointed the difference between vulgar show and elegance when he said, 'If John Bull turns around to look after you, you are not well dressed . . .'

Times change, as do stages. The modern stage for fashion was developed in the eighties. Clubs and discos were the places where fashion's *cognoscenti* congregated. As exclusive as the ballrooms of the past, they were almost as private. Dress rules, age limits and the personal preference of those running the occasion, ensured that only a certain section of society formed this world. Unlike the fashionable night world of the past, vulgarity and ostentation were not only permitted but actively encouraged. The successful appearance was the one that screamed 'look at me!' the loudest. It was all great fun for the young but, like the house parties and private balls of the past, represented an enclosed and private stage from which the majority was excluded.

The *real* stage for fashion now, a stage open to all at relatively small cost, is found in the pages of fashion magazines. With stylists and photographers as producers and directors, they create a long-running show that changes, if not nightly, then certainly every month. As if to acknowledge how artificial their role has become, fashion magazines increasingly feature clothes to be looked at but not worn. They place them in exotic surroundings, far removed from the background against which their readers wear clothes. Like a play, they even try to tell a story. The narrative element has become a major part of fashion coverage since it was first introduced in the early photo-essays of Bruce Weber in the late seventies and early eighties. As in Victorian fashion drawings, clothes are placed in a context. The context of fashion photographs is often bizarre and even disturbing. Again, like Victorian fashion illustrations, they have a strong class element and an even stronger erotic quality.

To look at the pages of a fashion magazine is frequently unsettling. Fashion's images have always been aimed at social voyeurs, but now they often seem to be aimed at sexual voyeurs too. The clothes are revealing, the poses lewd. The atmosphere has undertones of lesbianism and sadism. The narrative frequently shows the woman sexually menaced by rough-trade men in high-camp realisations of raw masculinity – the cowboy, the biker, or the bodybuilder. The message is a double one, complicated by the fact that the male 'actors' are usually manifestations of homosexual fantasies. The viewer's reaction is ambivalent: is the woman really being menaced, or is her very presence in fact menacing the men?

Flicking through such pages, we wonder to whom they are speaking. The answer is that they speak to us all – not directly, but through our subconscious. Like Surrealism, today's fashion magazines uncover our secret fears and desires whilst subliminally fuelling them. Helmut Newton's photographs demonstrated a long time ago the close links between pornography and fashion. Indeed, fashion coverage *is* pornography. The models are sexual fantasy objects. Whether showing clothes, make-up or hairstyles, they always appear to be on the verge of orgasm. But is it a sexual or a consumer climax? Or is it both? The pages of fashion magazines imply that buying is itself a form of orgasm; that possessing the latest goods produces an orgasm; that being looked at with envy is an orgasmic joy – all in addition to purely sexual orgasm.

In a world increasingly aware of the sexual menace that threatens females, with novels and films about serial killers, mutilators of female flesh and the torture and degradation of women enjoying huge popularity with both sexes, it is appropriate to ask how much fashion coverage has helped to distort our view of the roles and rites of men and women. Has the blatant display in fashion magazines of woman as sexual object, as something to be 'bought' as easily as her clothes – by coercion or force, if money is insufficient – cheapened female worth in the eyes of women as well as men?

That such questions are not asked, as they have been of novels, films and television programmes, is a clear indication of the intellectual downgrading of fashion by society. Intelligent people are not meant to take fashion or its magazines seriously. How easily we turn away with barely concealed irritation at 'ridiculous' prices, or outrageously extreme styles. It is this convenient and misguided dismissal of high fashion and its images that allows us to assume that fashion magazines and their approach to women have no effect on society. But fashion coverage that shows women as primarily sexual, even masturbatory, fantasy figures has had an effect upon how *all* women are viewed – an effect no less powerful because it is insidious; an effect no less dangerous because its medium is fashion, and perceived as harmless; an effect that influences not only how men see women but also how women see each other.

The fashion world is dominated by homosexuals of both sexes. It is not just exploitative of women, but also frequently misogynistic. Most male designers are gay, many stylists are lesbians and these designers and image-makers feed each other's fantasies. The eighties' revival of the mini is a good case in point. Although the mini might seem the quintessential garment of femininity, its actual effect is to change the female silhouette into a copy of that of the male. It is as near to masculine dress as a woman can achieve without wearing trousers. Tight and form-fitting, its paradox lies in the fact that, although it releases the legs, it restrains the thighs almost as the old-fashioned rubber corset did. It trammels whilst appearing to give freedom.

The genesis of the new mini is a confused one. It was not the creation of any one designer, although the thinking that made it possible had been done by Azzedine Alaïa. As early as the late seventies he was wrapping women tightly in short dresses of clinging jersey that followed and highlighted every contour of the body. But the mini was equally the creation of fashion editors and stylists who, perhaps to accommodate advertisers who had already observed that the age of the fashion consumer boom had dropped, were making their editorial pages appeal to the young woman. Stories of clothing being returned to manufacturers after photo sessions with as much as six inches lopped off the hem were legion – and not apocryphal – in the early eighties, as a trend was being established.

As the decade progressed, the mini on fashion pages and catwalks became more crudely sexy with each season. Balanced by broad-shouldered jackets, the silhouette grew less feminine every time until the fashionable young woman had been turned into a gay fantasy. Strong, aggressive, even menacing, she could have carried a whip instead of a handbag and it would have been perfectly in character. The outfit was black – the colour of authority and fear; the skirt was leather – the material of self-protection and cruel indifference to the individual. The new woman was the pastiche devil woman over whom gay designers fantasised and also the butch number over whom lesbian stylists fawned.

By the beginning of the nineties, bondage had become the new accessory and the mini had shrunk to a 'body', cut as revealingly as a swimming costume. Tight leggings and thigh-length jackets brought fashion back to the androgynous principal boy of pantomime, neither male nor female, but with an all-round appeal, able to be fancied by either sex. The process had taken about six years but was now complete. The fashionable woman was, once again, a sex object. Her retrogression had gone un-noted because it had been achieved in the apparently bland and unimportant pages of the fashion magazines considered so ridiculous by the intellectually pretentious.

EIGHT

Desirable Objects

Obscenity has no independent existence. It is a temporal, geographical and gender-based attitude of mind. What may be exposed on one continent must remain hidden on another. What may be worn today could have resulted in imprisonment or death in a previous century. Parts of the body which may be flaunted by males must remain hidden by females. Taboos are man made, but deeply ingrained. In Freud's words, 'At the root of every taboo there must be a desire.'

The conventional view of fashion history, written for the most part by men, is that whereas their sex was modest in dress, women were not. Breasts uncovered, shoulders lasciviously revealed, arms bared – the painters (also, in the main, men) have left us testimony to the sexuality of female dress. They have also left plenty of evidence of the far greater sexuality of male dress but, apart from the undeniable codpiece, we do not see it because our eyes are not trained to look at men as objects of sexual desire. This blindness stems from the historic approach we have taken to the dressed and undressed figure.

Sexuality is traditionally denoted by exposed flesh, by nudity, by nakedness. Few indeed are the paintings of nude men compared with those of women, and even those are usually of an allegorical or religious genre. Nude portraits are rare for either sex, but semi-nude portraits, where the sitter's fleshly beauty is to be admired above even clothes and surroundings, are very common – if they are portraits of women. Men are painted as they live, fully dressed. No off-the-shoulder or *décolleté* styles for them. This does not mean that women's dress is sexual and men's is not. Almost the exact opposite is the case.

Teenage boys and young men squeezed into skin-tight jeans or cycling pants quickly became a cliché of the eighties. They made a simple, albeit crude, statement about masculinity by exposing the buttocks and highlighting the genitals. Although not solely a male fashion (young women and girls wore their jeans just as tight, and to equal sexual effect), the masculine bulge made moralists particularly uneasy. Tight Lycra cycling pants outline the genitals quite specifically, in a way not previously seen in this century. However, such sexual display, clearly conceived to answer and outdo the female sexuality of the nipple pressed against the tight cotton T-shirt, was not new.

Chaucer's parson in the *Canterbury Tales* railed against the dress of fashionable young men in the fourteenth century because it exposed too much of the anatomy. As the hemlines of men's doublet grew shorter, they revealed the genitals in their hose in a way even more specific than the present cyclists' shorts. Although not an inch of flesh was exposed, the fashion flaunted the sex organs and showed 'the very boss of the penis and the horrible pushed-out testicles . . . and the buttocks of such persons look like the hinder part of a she-ape in the full of the moon.' Although young men of the time might not have gone so far as to foreshadow the pop stars who push shuttlecocks down their pants, the sexual effect of such dressing was just as calculated. The message was as obvious as that of the penis sheath worn by the Dani in New Guinea.

Like all bold and socially unsettling fashions that arose before the nineteenth century, doublets and coats were an aristocratic and courtly mode, as was the lasciviously pointed poulaine – the narrow shoe of the Middle Ages with strong phallic undertones in its shape. Condemned by a Papal Bull of 1468 as 'scoffing against God and the Church, a worldly vanity and a mad presumption', the poulaine was probably the world's first instant fashion sensation. It swept through the courts of Europe and, as Church and state criticism reached a climax, it became the 'must have' item for every fashionable upper-class young man. Quite apart from its evidence that men have the capacity to adore fashion and to dress to titillate just as much as women have, the poulaine shows that being a fashion victim has never been a state confined to the female sex. Not only were poulaines difficult to walk in, they were so narrow that they crippled the foot – just as did their re-run copies, the sixties' winklepickers. Such discomfort had no more effect on their popularity in the fourteenth century than it did in the twentieth.

But, of course, it does not do to mention such things. As the sociologist René König has observed, England is 'the birthplace of rampant puritanism', and men's dress is not meant to excite – or, indeed, to be attractive. As a foreigner, König politely refrained from mentioning another rampant English quality – hypocrisy. It is found at all levels and in all places. It is connived at by the very people who should expose it. In 1991 *The Independent on Sunday* allowed the Duchess of Devonshire to get away with calling herself a housewife, just like Mrs Jones next door – except that this particular housewife has, instead of the suburban pocket-handkerchief garden, a 1,000-acre deer park in a 36,000-acre estate. But this deceit, though symptomatic, is nothing compared with the hypocrisy we practise over clothes, our bodies and sexual attraction.

The comic Englishman amusingly delineated by Pierre Daninos in *Major Thompson* is an archetype still in existence today. So powerful is his image that the whole world has the same mental picture when the word 'Englishman' is spoken. It is of a grey-suited man, wearing a stiff-collared white shirt and a suitable tie. It is a uniform that confers anonymity on total nonentities and disguises their shortcomings. As such, it provides a safe cover for masculinity of all shapes and sizes. But when the same Englishman leaves his office, he slips into something altogether more casual. If he is a stockbroking 'whizz kid' he will be anxious to prove his street credibility by parading his Crolla shirt, Armani jeans and Paul Smith sweater as soon as he can. His off-duty clothes are as colourful as his girl-friend's, and they follow fashion quite as rigorously. Which dress reveals the true man, and which is the hypocrite's disguise? Is it possible that a man can feel equally at home in both forms of dress? If a wand could be waved would the City type happily go to work in his colourful off-duty clothes, or would he imagine that some of his mystique – and even some of his ability – had been removed along with the suitable suit? After all, a suit is something which falls in with requirements, something that pleases. The suit will never be discarded in business, simply because it gives its wearer an aura of power and probity – be he ne'er so hypocritical – beneath its uniform surface. Men need its mystique.

The suit also provides the stature and appearance of strength appropriate for leaders. With the exception of Henry VIII in his later days, the silhouette of power has always been one that carries no extra weight. Fat men are not taken seriously as leaders – although many become fat having attained their position whilst still commendably lean. The reason for this is atavistic. Out of 'the swirling mists of time' we subconsciously recall man the hunter, successful only if his body functioned efficiently. The suit of the twentieth-century male gives urban man the silhouette of the hunter – broad shouldered, narrow hipped and slim waisted. That the appearance is an illusion is a sign of the hypocrisy of clothing. Padding builds up and broadens a sagging shoulder-line; clever cut and skilful darting give the waist a smaller appearance. The result is that we see the hunter, alive and well, prowling Threadneedle Street and Wall Street in the assumed shape of his predacious ancestor.

The shape holds a great appeal for women. Not only do they enjoy the idea of the hunky he-man; they also want to assume his silhouette themselves. The eighties witnessed a fashion battle between the dress of youth, unstructured and loosely allowing the body to dominate the clothes, and that of maturity, with women's clothes building on and disguising an inadequate body just as the male suit does. Despite the hype surrounding the former and the adoration given to its great proponents – Galliano and Gigli – the latter won the day. Post-feminist women did not merely want the power of equality with men; they needed to share the dress of power. Hugely padded shoulders gave women the silhouette of the hunter and broad, tight belts made them appear lithe and efficient, like killer cats. Disparagingly dubbed 'Dynasty' or 'Dallas' dressing, it affected an enormous number of women. By their dress, they wished to assume the glamour of Joan Collins – whose clothes on or off the screen exemplified her role, in fiction and in fact, as the powerful woman in charge of herself and her men – and to appropriate the style of the Princess of Wales, elegant, sophisticated and apparently unrufflable.

The twentieth century has been called the century of svelte, but it was only in the eighties that slimness and power came together to fulfil the definition. The leader of the 'slimness equals power' movement was Nancy Reagan. As First Lady of America, her fashion influence was immense – not merely in her own country but across the world. It is easy to dismiss Mrs Reagan, as most fashion commentators have, as a pathological fashion freak, but it is wrong to do so. It was her sophisticated urban dressing that gave women a confidence-boosting role model. Her formal approach to clothes convinced many women at high street level that, although the young appeared to have all the advantages, the one thing they could not achieve was elegance – and that was what gave older women the dignity to compete with men. Without the real-life Mrs Reagan and the understated class of her designer dressing, would Joan Collins and her vulgarisation of the look have had any hope of succeeding as a high-street influence?

Mrs Reagan instigated a new approach to dress but, more than that, she exerted a cultural influence. From her impeccably cut example sprang the new class of New York socialite, the designer darling. Elegant women who devoted their lives to fashionable New York society were not new. What changed their status in the early eighties was the elevation of the Fairchild fortnightly publication W into virtually their house magazine, and the coincidental arrival of Nancy Reagan in the White House. A group of rather foolish, obsessive and incestuously inward-looking women, for whom the world outside their wealthy enclave hardly existed, was so avidly followed and reported by W that it became a movement, and was even dignified with a title. The expression 'the ladies who lunch' might well have been coined as a put-down for these women who believed that the only true use for wealth was to spend it self-indulgently on oneself, but it had a snob cachet recognised far from the favoured tables of La Grenouille or the other Manhattan watering holes they graced with their elaborately traditional appearance.

Under their aegis, the decent obscurity with which wealth self-protectively shrouds itself was swept away by the new vulgarity which said, 'If you've got it, flaunt it – and make sure that W is there to record the moment.' The leaders of this strange movement – among them Nan Kempner, Pat Buckley, Judy Peabody, Nancy Kissinger and Annette Reed – did not exactly become household names, but they were certainly better known than their true worth merited. For they were little more than designer mannequins in an animated *Théâtre de la Mode*, dancing for the media as they unflaggingly attended a gruelling round of occasions called social but actually nearer to showbiz. The charity dinners, the art gallery openings, the fund-raising bashes meant not a thing. It was the clothes that counted – and the photographers who gave them their fix through good old-fashioned personal publicity.

The ladies who lunch are nothing more than living Barbie dolls. Like Barbie, their one purpose is to wear a wardrobe which is to be changed as frequently as possible. Barbie is a fantasy doll, who has no meaning without her clothes. She trains little girls to know that their role is to dress 'fancy' in order to be the personification of male fantasies: clean, dumb and available. Barbie is the Hugh Heffner nightmare come true: airbrushed (she has no navel or nipples) and antiseptic (she cannot sweat and never smells), just as his *Playboy* magazine suggests men wish women to be.

The idea of a woman of Pat Buckley's age as a Barbie doll may not be easy to stomach – until you see her and her society sisters in an Ungaro evening dress or a Valentino cocktail number. Then it all becomes clear. Forget the face. Everything else is perfect. Expensively packaged, the ladies who lunch have one function, just like Barbie: they are to be admired because of their wardrobe. This is where their influence is so great. They have affected fashion because, thanks to *W*, they are high profile. Big bucks glamour dressing is their *raison d'être*. The designers who wish to become rich design big bucks glamour clothing, knowing that the 200,000 women who read *W*, the out-of-town movers and shakers of fashion, want to look like Pat Buckley and the girls. It has been estimated that for designers chasing this lucrative market, a credit in a social report in *W* is worth more than a $30,000 colour-page advertisement in American *Vogue*.

Probably the most lasting effect of the ladies who lunch has been their influence on designers, not merely in fashion terms, but in personal kudos. They have made certain of them, such as Bill Blass, Oscar de la Renta and Valentino, not just socially acceptable, but socially desirable. Bill Blass is invited to every New York party, Oscar de la Renta visits China with Henry Kissinger, Valentino is a friend of Agnelli; they – and many other designers – mix socially with their clients. In this, they have brought fashion round full circle, back to the days when Worth was social arbiter and Poiret behaved with more grandeur than even his most aristocratic clients. The kings of fashion dine with the queens of fashionable life, whilst the dauphins – such as the upwardly mobile Italian designer Versace – struggle desperately to join their number. All believe themelves sufficiently important to produce *ex-cathedra* pronouncements. Be it Armani suggesting, in a phrase that patronises an entire sex, that he wishes his clothes to make women think, or Versace, in a particularly pernicious piece of special pleading on behalf of his clients, averring that 'Luxury is part of civilisation. It is a gift from the Gods,' or even Arabella Pollen, denying her craft with the peculiarly British hypocrisy that has made London a fashion backwater, declaring ' . . . I think it is stupid to be governed by fashion. It's relatively unimportant and certainly should never be taken seriously,' the pronouncements are pretentious and banal. Vacuous and hypocritical as such remarks are, they are part of the stock in trade of the modern designer who feels too important merely to make clothes, but feels that he must moralise and philosophise about them and the women who wear them.

Dress designers have always been neurotically arrogant – even in the days when the rules of taste imposed a form of fashion consistency in a way not unlike that of the informed aristocratic eye which produced the perfection of eighteenth-century architecture. They are even more so now that the rules of taste have been swept away. Style has become the criterion for *not* judging fashion and merely allowing designers to create what they feel is right, the fashion world having forgotten that the Biblical definition of anarchy is doing that which is right in one's own eyes. When there are no rules, there are no absolute standards, there can be no judging and any upstart prince can seize the crown. Andy Warhol, extreme exponent of the 'do it wrong and make a bomb' approach to creativity, showed the way – not because he did not know how to do it right but because he knew that he could rely on the art world not knowing or, perhaps, not caring. In many respects, the fallout of his cynical approach has influenced fashion – the most susceptible of creative forces – more than any other field. If a person considers himself a king, or even a crown prince, he behaves with an assurance that can easily slip over into arrogance. As Karl Lagerfeld – a designer whose clothes and personality do not always please New York's designer darlings – has explained in *W*, it is easy for fashion designers to take themselves too seriously: 'Twenty years ago they were still trade persons . . . They should all be happy that people pay them so much attention. After rock stars and a few movie stars . . . they make more money than anybody else.' But of course, when you have a certain amount, making more becomes almost inevitable and the satisfaction lessens. Something else is needed. Whereas the ladies who lunch play at charity, world-famous mega-wealthy designers play at being aristocrats, amassing grand houses and expensive art collections to give themselves a cultural credibility that distances them from their trade, precisely as the newly ennobled aristocracy did in the early eighteenth century. Sadly, as they are almost all homosexual, they are neither founding dynasties nor collecting for their children's grandchildren, as was the case with their aristocratic forerunners: it is an exercise in purely personal aggrandisement.

The homosexuality that dominates the world of fashion has transformed the big-bucks dressing of the early eighties into something close to misogyny for the early nineties. The problem starts with the designer's ideal of the female figure, which is the adolescent boy's shape with the addition of breasts. As most top models have the adolescent boy's shape without breasts, they increasingly have the deficiency made up for them, using silicone. These synthetic breasts have little in common with real breasts. Whereas the real things are, as one feminist describes them, 'rawly natural' and move with their own rhythm as the body moves, the silicone jelly sacks of the breast implants worn by an estimated 80 per cent of top models are rigid and have none of this movement. Many homosexual designers are repulsed by female breasts as the outward and visible sign of the motherhood which destroys the perfection of the female figure even as it menaces their own sexual world. As far as they are concerned, artificial, predictable and controllable silicone versions are far preferable. The caricature of a woman's body that results from implanted breasts sitting awkwardly on slender frames devoid of other curves is a mortification of female flesh, and contemptuous of woman's natural shape.

If homosexual designers are afraid of breasts, they hide their fear in laughter, by making fun of them and the femininity they signify. Conical bras, outrageously pointed and bearing no relationship to the shape of real breasts, are a cruel joke that bring women into the world of the crudest female impersonators and put them on the same level as the rugby player with coconuts under his jersey. Amazingly, a section of the female fashion world has taken them seriously and Madonna has worn them almost as cult objects, if not to universal approval then neither to the condemnation that might have been expected. For homosexual designers to mock femininity is one thing, but when women join in the mirth at this crass parodying of their sex, it raises different issues. The sting is not removed simply because the laughter is female.

Or is Madonna perhaps laughing at the pathetic lubricity of men? By slipping off her kimono at the 1991 Cannes Film Festival to reveal her fifties-style bra and corset, was she guying the female stereotype of underpinnings to glamour and how men manipulated women into such straits? Or was she demonstrating, albeit crudely, the power of the female in charge of herself, her sexuality and the men who cluster around her? We are so used to the stereotype of the woman as pawn to male lewdness – the victim who sprawls orgasmically across the bonnet of the phallic sports car – that it is difficult to imagine that some women might be strong enough to play the game in order to turn the man into the victim. Is Madonna, bound and trussed in tight bra, laced corset and boots, ready to be skewered for the delectation of men? Or is she showing her male admirers how unnecessary they are by getting off on her own self-inflicted torture? Her dress is frequently ambivalent, containing the elements of both the tight-laced down-trodden Victorian wife of popular imagination – the bride stripped bare of all but her chains – and the dominatrice, ready to brandish her whip and humiliate man, the worm, whilst he sweats with desire for the heaving breasts pushed forward by her bra as a delectable feast perpetually beyond his power. Her appearance has a strength that transcends wealth and masculinity and creates its own archetype. It says, 'Fuck you', to all the men who want to hear, 'Fuck me'.

For women less in control than Madonna, the nubile figure has, over the last fifty years, become the dumb figure. In its original sense, nubility meant marriageability; now it stands for a voluptuous curvaceousness that fashion disdains. Designers consider the full figure vulgar, even though they find it rather exciting. They love the pulchritude of Jayne Mansfield and Marilyn Monroe, whose curves suggested that with their bodies women can, almost literally, swamp men – but they have no desire to design for them. Their admiration is based in laughter and they take themselves far too seriously to laugh at their own creativity. But by denying the validity of natural female curves they have not merely made a fashion statement; they have developed an attitude which is dangerous to the whole of society. The reason young women suffer from anorexia and bulimia is cultural. To be fat is not merely to be unfashionable. So powerful is fashion and the obsessions of its leaders that to be fat has come to be seen as a manifestation of stupidity and laziness. The fat person cannot be fashionable not just because she is the 'wrong' shape, but because she is a slob.

This attitude is the result of the idealised concept of woman, designed by the *couturier*, disseminated by the media and desired by all. A fat woman, it is assumed, has no standards. Not only is she lazy, she is probably sluttish and is clearly ignorant. In an unspoken but real sense, she is seen as not being contemporary, and is therefore contemptible in the eyes of fashion which is, by definition, nothing if not that.

Whereas *couturiers* in the past created clothes with real customers and their physical deficiencies in mind, modern designers create in the abstract for a ready-to-wear mass market which has, as its ideal image, the impossible figure of the top model – the frame of an adolescent boy with the addition of static, dense breasts. Designers decide that women should look that way and fashionable women do their best to make sure that they live up to the decree. Apart from the breasts, no awkward lumps or uncontrolled flesh must be allowed to destroy the silhouette.

The result is a baleful one. For most women in the Western world losing weight is a permanent obsession, constantly fuelled by the almost inevitable sense of failure that spurs them on. Their ideal body weight image – ruthlessly pushed at them in the pages of glossy magazines – is at least ten pounds less than the prevailing norm: and yet they still try. Their greatest praise for another woman is a reward for this perseverance: 'You look marvellous; you've lost weight!' Fat women, they convince themselves into agreeing with the designers, cannot look sexy. Fashion reflects and creates society's obsessions. Just like her early Victorian counterpart, the young woman of today as she nears her thirties frequently becomes obsessed with marriage. Non-sexy women do not attract men and do not marry, so the myth goes. They therefore diet, because the pangs of hunger are nothing compared with the fear of becoming that lonely, splintery, thorny creature – the spinster. While the term 'old maid' is deliberately and pejoratively insulting, 'spinster' does not appear to have the same connotations – and yet it possesses a coldly dismissive ring entirely lacking in the word 'bachelor'. It denotes feminine failure in society's eyes.

Career women defend their pursuit of slimness – as they do their pursuit of high fashion – as a necessary conforming to the expectations of a job market dominated by male standards. After all, they argue, men are the hirers. But the argument falls down when women become the hirers. Almost always, they hire a mirror image of themselves – an idealised figure, fashionable (but not outrageously so), slim and well made-up – that exactly fulfils the male criteria. Any woman who deviates from the expected image does so at her peril. Of the thousands of authenticated cases of professional victimisation suffered by women as a result of their looks (a thing unheard of in the history of men at work) all are instigated by men who have their own idea of glamour and how women should appear, and how that appearance suggests a woman should act in a male-dominated world. The ideal, in every case, has begun on the designer's catwalk, usually many seasons previously. It will not be too fashionable (most men are afraid of women in high fashion dress), but it will be slim – after all, 'Fat Slags' to be laughed at are found in *Viz*, the comic that appeals to men, not women.

Nabokov's novel *Lolita* appeared in Paris in 1955. It was privately printed and New York had to wait until 1958 for publication. The London publication came a year later. It altered society's view of both youth and sexuality. It was one of the events that changed attitudes sufficiently to enable the miniskirt to be accepted when it came along. There are no absolutes in dress. Although modesty appears as a permanent aspect of our psyche its manifestations alter in response to modified attitudes. The sixties' mini would have had the wearer arrested in the twenties and yet, compared with the late eighties' mini, it seems innocent. Late eighties' – early nineties' minis are a far cry from the woman as baby girl that Quant and Courreges produced. They are now about naked – or semi-naked – power. They make a woman look as fit for command and ready to control as any man. Equally as important, they highlight the difference between youth and age that first became a fashion issue with the original mini.

Young legs can be lovely, old legs cannot. That the mini in its second coming has been confined to the young probably shows nothing more significant than the fact that the women who went through it first time round are too wise to be caught out a second time. For women in their mid thirties to imagine that they can bridge the credibility gap by wearing a short skirt is absurd and is seen as such by most. Not every middle-aged woman can be a Tina Turner – nor would the majority wish to be. Like Madonna, Turner stands for many things. Male fantasies of being overwhelmed by the Jungle Woman, as implacable as she is insatiable, are balanced by female dreams of being tauntingly in charge of one's body and behaviour in a male-structured world. Both stars point to the future. Already, women's dress parades a blatant sexuality previously unknown. The paradox is that it frightens as many men as it excites.

As we said earlier, the second-coming mini, worn with a tailored jacket, gives women a male silhouette whilst highlighting their femininity. The appearance is perversely contradictory, as is its effect on the onlooker. A body so exposed seems vulnerable and yet the wearer is clearly in charge of her self and her world. Whereas the sixties' mini was in the pastel shades of the nursery and worn with flat heels, the eighties' mini is in the colours of the boardroom, occasionally enlivened by the guardsman's scarlet. Whereas the old mini was a dress, the new mini is a skirt. Flick through any fashion magazine and it becomes immediately apparent: women wear suits just as men do – and for the same reason. A minidress is demeaning to femininity; a miniskirt, with jacket and high heels, is enhancing to female power – and thus frightening to men. Helen Storey, the English designer, summed up the position from the female point of view. 'A Laura Ashley smock which spells the subservient woman locked prettily in her place is far more frightening than black plastic boots.' Most liberated women would agree. Dresses denote domesticity in a way that a surrogate suit never could.

Young women who imagined themselves in charge of their lives wore increasingly short, tight and 'sexy' clothes during the eighties. They did so for a variety of reasons. They saw the glamour of Mrs Reagan and the ladies who lunch – and they wanted it; they imagined the sex life of Joan Collins and the cast of *Dynasty* – and they wanted it; they realised the power of the City-suited male – and they wanted it; they saw the slackness of the tracksuit – and they did *not* want it. The tracksuit's genesis was not part of the new woman's sex and power formula. It had two main disadvantages: it was a central prop of the complicated semiotics of teenage dress, and it carried the non-status informality of the council estate and the disadvantaged ethnic group. Tight, sexy, short clothing was its antithesis, the uniform of the upwardly mobile woman, dressed in the sleek sheath of success. This was not just the phallic woman bucking for power, it was the woman with balls, the woman who, given half a chance, could annihilate most of the men who stood in the way of her ambition. If, at times, it was inconvenient and uncomfortable, that was not important. Status dress has been so since the sixteenth century.

Fashion is a process of cross-fertilisation, from salon to street and back again. Designers understood the new mood of confidence and began to produce designs that enhanced it. Power dressing had moved beyond *Dallas* and the television screen to become a reality of the streets. Narcissism is one of mankind's oldest and most absorbing obsessions and, as the nineties dawned, women fell for it anew. The reflection that thrilled them was a heady mix of female allure and male power. It straddled both worlds and created a hybrid stronger than both. The new way of dressing betokened the new confidence.

The Pill appeared in 1963. Its effect on clothes was quickly seen. Baby Doll dresses symbolised women's reaction to the sort of sexuality they felt men required at the time: sex when the man made the decision, but *control* held by the woman. The pill gave a sexual freedom with which the condom could not compete and the minidress was the uniform of that freedom, giving men easier access than had ever been known. Women could play the game of compliancy because they had the pill.

The eighties' equivalent of the pill was the shock of Aids. With governments insisting that the condom must be reinstated, the balance between control and availability again altered just as dramatically as it had in the sixties. The cataclysmic shift was clothed in sexually specific garb: the mini, the litmus paper of sexual mores, appeared once more. Like its first coming, it was worn in defiance. The pill had opened the door for sexual freedom, the mini had proclaimed the fact. Aids appeared to close the door, and the new mini proclaimed that fact. But appearance is not always reality. All that had actually changed was that control reverted to the male. Or rather, control of the *how* of sex had reverted, but not the when or the who. Women held these two vital cards. And they dressed to show it in clothes that encouraged masturbatory fantasies rather than close encounters of a real kind.

The nineties have started on a note of hope. Women are more sure of themselves, socially and sexually, than they have ever been. They wear the trappings of S&M and bondage with the same authority as they were worn by the punks who first brought them out of the sexual twilight zone of the specialist club. Even nice girls are prepared to be thought of as raunchy – as the pages of *Vogue* make clear. Like Tina Turner and, above all, Madonna, they have discovered the sexual thrill of tantalisation. 'Look, squirm, pant with desire,' they say to men, 'but you cannot touch.' How men respond to the new challenge – and what response women will then make – will decide how the sexes move into the new century. It is an open question – eight years is a long time in fashion. What is certain, however, is that the evolution of new roles will be first signified by dress.

THE LURE
OF LINGERIE

When fashion is in the doldrums it falls back on paradox. Men's clothing is shown as women's fashion; the rules of taste are flouted; underwear is suggested as outerwear – a look championed by Jean-Paul Gaultier and Vivienne Westwood. In some cases the designer's hand is crude but John Galliano's slip dress, from his 'Josephine Napoleon meets Lolita' collection for Spring 1992, has taste, delicacy and charm. This fashion approach, like Horst's photograph of silk stockings, shows that, with skill and artistry, sex does not have to be salacious.

HAVING FUN

A fashion show by the French designer Thierry Mugler is always stimulating but, behind the excitement of his fantasies, it is difficult to see what there is for women to actually wear. Conversely, a show by a 'street cred' designer like London's Katherine Hamnett is frequently so banal that the looks on the catwalk are very similar to those worn by the audience, and must be presented outrageously in order to be noticed at all.

POWER PACKS

In American football the power of the player is what counts. Dressed like an armoured medieval knight, the footballer thunders down the field, his body entirely encased in protective clothing. His broad shoulders, narrow waist and Gaultier-codpiece lacing give him an appearance so extreme that it is a pastiche of masculinity. English football is so heavily sponsored that players are now running, jumping, kicking advertisements, as much as they are sportsmen.

DECLINE AND FALL

Fashion feeds on flesh whilst trying to ignore its frailties. When youth and beauty turn to age and ugliness, fashion averts its gaze, revolted at what has happened. It punishes the woman who will not let go by making her grotesque - the ultimate fate of the fashion victim.

CHAPTER OPENING IMAGES

PICTURE CREDITS

Index